A Dynasty of Clergy named Archer

Graham Claydon

Published by

MELROSE BOOKS

An Imprint of Melrose Press Limited
St Thomas Place, Ely
Cambridgeshire
CB7 4GG, UK
www.melrosebooks.co.uk

FIRST EDITION

Copyright © Graham Claydon 2018

The Author asserts his moral right to
be identified as the author of this work

Cover designed by Melrose Books

**ISBN   978-1-912026-79-1 paperback
        978-1-912026-80-7 epub
        978-1-912026-81-4 mobi**

Printed and bound in Great Britain by:
Airdrie Print Services Ltd
24-26 Floweerhill Street
Airdrie, North Lanarkshire
Scotland, ML6 6BH

Contents

Foreword

This is a study of five generations of clergy of the Church of England whom I originally came across when researching my own family. I soon realised that I had stumbled across a wealth of information about five characters born in very different times and a variety of social and political situations. There are no published books about any of them, although each finds a mention somewhere in a contemporary publication. But beyond those passing references, their story had to be painstakingly dug up from a wide variety of material, necessitating a good deal of scholarly peregrination as well as more sedentary searches online.

The story starts as the role of a minister or priest was being redefined. Prior to the Reformation, their task was primarily sacramental – taking masses, hearing confessions, baptising, and burying. Some of these roles survived the changes in the church, although multiple masses were replaced by occasional Communions, and daily services became briefer, leaving more time for other tasks. What those tasks were emerges from the Archers' story in each generation, so that by the end we will have followed the evolution of the role of a parish priest over three hundred years.

At an early stage in my own task, I was fortunate enough to come across a network of historians who were working on assembling a database that gathered together a record of every clergyman ordained in the Church of England from the time of the Reformation until the reign of Victoria. Their work involved ploughing through Ordination and Visitation Registers over the entire period. But it has been achieved, although fine-tuning continues. Initially, this was raw data from which to understand the shaping of the English church more fully. In particular, my thanks go to two members of the project – Dr Ken Fincham of Canterbury University, who read and commented so helpfully on my manuscript; and Dr Andrew Foster of Chichester, who did the same and also welcomed me into a community of friends, each of whom was in some way or another involved in exploring more about the historic church. I also had contact with my ex-tutor from King's College London days, Professor Patrick Collinson, who sadly died before I went to publication. But beyond specific names, I wish to thank the army of archivists who either online or in person have been so gracious in answering my questions and suggesting avenues to go down.

Historical knowledge may sometimes seem a minority interest, although fascination with the past seems written into the human psyche. This study brings newly-researched material for the historian, along with the stories of five clergy who, it is to be hoped, will be of interest to those with a wide interest in the stories of our ancestors and all they got up to. The breadth of the period covered by these five lives gives us ample opportunity to reflect on the nature of a clergyman's role in society. Jokes about working only one day a week still persist, but this is in part because there is an ignorance of the clergyman's role in everyday life. This study will go some way towards enabling us to decide how much the role of a priest changes from generation to generation, and how much a core brief remains unchanged from one century to the next.

By observing the general patterns of each Archer story, we may expect to outline more exactly what it is that a clergyman does. The overall story spans 250 years, and another 250 have passed since that time, in which major changes have occurred in society and the church, which in turn demand subsequent examination. I will leave it to the reader to reflect on how much of the core values of the post-Reformation clergy still remain in modern times. To aid that reflection, I have written an introductory chapter that examines some of the issues running through the story, and also looks into sources which are so critical in reconstructing the five biographies that comprise the rest of the book.

Introduction

"Biography in almost all literary traditions has been seen as the
most vivid sort of history one can write. It personalises history, it
centres history on individuals, it encapsulates history in a number of
individual lives." *Tarif Khaldi, Images of Mohammed.*[1]

A study of Mohammed may not be the most likely quote to head an
historical study of Church of England clergy, but I happened to be
reading it at the same time I was writing up the Archer story and it
stood out as expression of the universal pull towards biography in our
search to understand history. Of course, there is history that cannot be
explained by biography as well as biography that plays fast and loose
with history.

One contention of this book is that the clergy generally became
attached to the gentry class, which invites another relevant quote from
Adam Nicholson in his book on the gentry:

"Any examined group tended to fragment into its individuals and
blur all possible definitions. In the aftermath of 'The Storm over the
Gentry' historians have retreated from large-scale theorising towards
closer descriptions of individual families."[2]

The success of the TV programme *Who do you think you are?* has
been a further contribution to understanding history from the stories
of our ancestors, in which family history and general history become
two sides of the same coin. There has always been a suspect side to
genealogy, since it has often been bound up with the pursuit of social
status. The current renewal of interest in family history is hopefully
freer of this twist. It so happens that clergy have played a significant

role in the world of genealogy as guardians of the parish registers that provide us with the most basic facts of our ancestors' existence – births, marriages, and deaths. Furthermore, since the traditional country parish did not always fill a clergyman's time and given that they had more ready access to church and college records than the average person in society, for many of them both history and genealogy became a hobby. There is no evidence that any of the Archer family took a particular interest in their ancestry although they were acutely aware of it, especially when it might help them obtain a job!

Of course, there have been thousands of clergy, of which only a small number have found their way into the history books. The majority of these are the "higher clergy". Most bishops have an entry in the ODNB.[3] Others became entangled in politics, some were also writers, philosophers, scientists, historians, and poets. A few were rogues whose scandals made them notorious, and some were so eccentric that their stories have survived. But the vast majority lived relatively humble, everyday lives, unless disturbed and displaced by political and social upheavals. Paradoxically, times of upheaval often provide us with more information than the more tranquil periods of our history. The exception to this pattern comes from everyday clerical diaries of which only a handful remain in print: *The Diary of Ralph Josselin* in the 17th century, and *Woodforde's Diary*[4] a century later, are two of the richest, along with the more dramatic journals of John Wesley and George Whitfield, which were designed to be printed and widely distributed.[5] Many clerical stories have been preserved anecdotally, often in the localities in which a vicar lived and worked, where they endure in local histories. There are also more general studies of the clergy in these periods that are illustrated with examples from the lives of individual ministers, notably in the writings of A. Tindal Hart.[6]

A more imaginative source of clerical information comes from the growth and spread of the novel, featuring a wide range of clergy, from Fielding's Parson Adams to Trollope's Archdeacon Grantly. The frequency with which clergy appear in novels reflects the fact that they were woven into the social fabric of the times, so that a story set in England would be hard to write without some appearance of a parish priest. Whilst the clergy took themselves seriously on the whole, novelists had an eye to their eccentricities and saw them as vehicles of comic relief as well as pillars of society. Of course, many novelists were themselves clergy or, like Jane Austen, resided in a clergy household. Novels can therefore be a rich seam of information about the church and clergy. However, we need to remember that they are artistic creations in which clergy may be presented as figures of fun, hypocrites, or romantic heroes.

It may be impossible to entirely disassociate ourselves from these fictional masterpieces, but in telling this story I have sought to be strictly governed by the available historic sources pertinent to the one clergy family I have selected. It is an exploration of five generations of a family named Archer, beginning in 1588 and ending in 1832. The choice of this family was initially circumstantial, connected to my own genealogical explorations. Soon I was meeting their many clergy friends and relatives, and building up a broader picture of clergy families. Often these families were established around a particular parish where the family had obtained the right of appointment or "advowson". Often this passed from father to son for a generation or two, but then was given to a cousin or nephew or just a family friend. What makes the Archers stand out is the absence of such an advowson; each generation had to find its own way into a parish, even when there were family connections to help. Furthermore, for these five generations the clerical vocation consistently passed from father to son without a break.

I was initially pessimistic about finding sufficient sources for all five generations of Archers, since I had already worked out that many clergy left very little behind them that could provide a portrait of their lives in any detail. But I need not have worried! Generation by generation, the basic outline of their lives emerged with many surprises and some humour, too! So, at this point I will set out the sources that made the overall stories possible. Some will be repeated in the later text, and some more detailed by footnotes. But now I offer the story of the sources, which in turn provide framework for exploring other clergy histories.

First came the online CCEd – The Clergy of the Church of England Database, which aims to record the basic information about every Church of England priest ordained from 1540 until the appearance of *Crockford's Clerical Dictionary* in 1837. Within those 297 years, all clergy should have had their ordination and appointments recorded in the Bishops' Register, from which they have been transferred to the database. How fully these registers have survived will eventually become clear, but the signs are that the majority have done so. The Archer entries seem to be pretty well complete, though Edward's ordinations are presumed to be on pages of the Bishops' Register that have been irreparably damaged. The database is now sufficiently advanced to provide the foundation for more detailed studies of individual clergy. Prior to the database, checking information could be time-consuming and involve many trips to scattered diocesan archives.

Since most clergy of this period attended Oxford or Cambridge, university and college records usually supply names, father, dates, academic achievements, and sometimes appointments. All the Archers appear in university registers. There are sometimes amplified accounts of students in college histories, particularly for those who became Fellows. Thus, Charles Boase's excellent study of Exeter College, Oxford,[7] gives plentiful information about Benjamin Archer and what was happening around him in the 1670s. School records are scant, and only Thomas the elder's schooling can be traced from Eton records.

There was a brief period in our study when the Church was taken over by Parliament during the Interregnum, and record-keeping was more hit and miss, reflecting ever-changing directives from the top. There are nevertheless records for this time that may be found in the

Calendar of State Papers Domestic (CSPD) or the records of parliamentary committees. There is an invaluable Commonwealth Register in the British Library which lists clergy appointments in the 1650s. New work is being undertaken about parliamentary appointments by the Ejectors and Triers in the 1650s in which Edward Archer's name has come to light.

From 1538, every clergyman was required to maintain a parish register in which he was to enter every birth, marriage, and death in his parish. Some reading between the lines can be done, and occasionally the parson sees fit to add some comments of his own! In addition to the registers, the parish kept records of expenditure and significant decisions or plans for the future. These have partly survived in the churchwardens' accounts. Here, too, it is often the incidental name or comment that gives a window into the life of a parish and its parson.

Clergy were inveterate letter writers, of which some have survived. Many clergy wrote their sermons out in full and many were published. Some have survived. Reformation clergy emerged from their university training as historians, classicists, linguists, mathematicians, and musicians – as well as theologians. In their country parishes, they continued to read, write books, poetry, letters, and diaries; some grew fascinated by the questions raised by science, and joined in the new interest in observing, measuring, weighing, and recording nature. Others pursued history, wrote about the ancient and recent past, and explored their own ancestry.

The consequence of their literary pursuits is that we have a wealth of clerical writings even after the ravages of time have destroyed much of this rich legacy. The results, however, are patchy: many database clergy leave hardly any other mark of their existence. Others leave much that is somewhat turgid, and adds little to our understanding of the person or his calling. The Archers left quality rather than quantity. Edward's tract is in the William Salt Library and many American Universities!

Benjamin's letters are in the British Library. Thomas senior contributed to Wilford's Lives, and edited Marshall's sermons. Thomas junior was either the most prolific or the best preserved. Many of his poems can be traced in the British Library, Gentleman's Magazine, and Essex Record Office, whilst his letters are at Eton and the British Library. Thus, all the Archers have left personal writings, with the exception of James.

Of all clerical writings, letters and diaries can be the most rewarding sources. A letter brings a person alive over the centuries. Letters are most likely to have survived by reaching the archive of a significant person whose collection of documents is still kept in their ancestral home, or has been passed to a Record Office for preservation. Benjamin's extant letters were written to Hans Sloane, and preserved in the Sloane collection. Thomas junior wrote to Lord Hardwicke, Eton College, and the Prime Minister, all of whom preserved their correspondence. Some letters remain in families and await their journey to a record office for safekeeping and public access. Diaries are few and far between, compared with letters. There are no Archer diaries, but some more famous surviving diaries, like that of Anthony Wood,[8] gossip about people so widely that two generations of Archers get mentioned! And whilst no Archers are mentioned directly in Woodforde's diary, their mutual friends, the Bodhams, are.

Wills can be windows into souls. In part formulaic, they can nevertheless be quite personal and provide an overview of the values and concerns of someone whose perceptions are sharpened by realising that they have little time to live. It was not unusual for early modern wills to include a re-affirmation of the faith in which the deceased departed this life, and clergy wills were almost expected to be doctrinally correct in every way. Each Archer will has a theological introduction about faith and salvation that may be slightly differently worded, but essentially affirms the reformation doctrine of justification by faith. Edward's wife Mary includes an affirmation of the doctrine of the Trinity for good measure, since the wives, too, were theologically literate.

Wills also provide a good deal of wide-ranging family information from their various bequests. The Archer wills were proved in the Prerogative Court of Canterbury, in spite of being modest affairs. Only Ann Archer's will was proved in the local Archdeaconry Court. This study is enriched by the existence of five Archer wills, each illuminating the times and personality of the deceased, namely: Mary 1686; Benjamin 1732; Ann 1733; Thomas 1767; and Thomas 1832. Although Edward died intestate, there was an Administration that provided many details about his domestic circumstances, including the first mention of an Archer library. The other invaluable information surrounding death comes from memorials. These exist, or have existed, for Benjamin and his wife, and both Thomases in Quainton, Hitcham and Foulness.

In comparison, legal cases and land documents can be dry, but their information is often significant. An insight into James comes from his presenting a case to the local quarter Sessions. For Edward, it was a tithe dispute that started locally and found its way to London that presents a vivid record of his parishioners recalling what they remembered of his ministry at Newington. Then the Archers were involved in the division of a family estate through their mother's inheritance. An indenture provides details about all their relatives at that time, whilst the flurry of letters and tenancy agreements made at the end of the younger Thomas's life remind us that without pensions a clergyman needed to provide for their widow and unmarried daughters, in particular. Indeed, these letters, although not personal, nevertheless paint a picture of economic circumstances and additional sources of income. When Woods, long-time solicitors in Rochford, closed down, their papers were fortunately handed to the Southend Record Office. Meanwhile, Thomas's uncle went bankrupt and his affairs were unravelled by the House of Lords and recorded in their Journal.

Towards the end of the period, local newspapers were spreading and both the *Cambridge Chronicle* and the *Chelmsford Chronicle* tell us more about the younger Thomas and his scandalous elopement! More dignified are the pages of *The Gentleman's Magazine*, which reports appointments and deaths, and in which Thomas junior had published some of his poems. Most surprising of all was coming across a catalogue of printers in which the marriage of Mary Dixon – the mother of Thomas junior – was described at length, since this first marriage was to a bookseller.

My first clue to this long-running clergy family began with a family paper, which took me in search of a Reverend Thomas Archer and any records about him in the then Southend Record Office, which in turn led to the more prestigious archives of Eton College. There I came across a letter in their Hitcham papers from the Revd. Thomas Archer, dated 8 December, 1810. It was sent from Southchurch Parsonage near Rochford, Essex, and was addressed to: "The Revd. And worthy society, the Provost, Vice-Provost, and Fellows of Eton College". The letter contained the claim that: "all my ancestors (as I have understood) were clergymen for the space of many generations".

I became curious as to how many generations that might prove to be, and by diligently working back I concluded that the Thomas Archer was the fifth generation to be ordained in a line that clipped the edge of Elizabeth's reign and continued a few years short of Victoria, nearly 250 years later. It would of course be possible to pack five generations into half that time but generally it seems that because clergy underwent many years of study and then had to find a living that would support a family, they ended up marrying late and becoming more mature parents than the average member of society. Unfolding the story of each generation chronologically means that there will inevitably be some overlap between the generations. In effect this results in hearing first from the father, and subsequently seeing some of the same events from the viewpoint of the child.

Clergy families only began to come back into being after the Reformation. Celibacy had been normative in Christendom for several hundred years, even if the presence of concubines and clerical bastards was tolerated. Archbishop Cranmer, we know, married secretly since his reformed faith led him to believe in clerical matrimony, but he feared the State's ongoing support for some Catholic doctrines, including celibacy. Cranmer had children who were not happy people, since they must have felt that their father hid them away and was ashamed of them. Knowing that many Roman Catholic beliefs lingered on into Elizabeth's reign and beyond, there must have been many who frowned at the rise of the clergy family. Indeed, Queen Elizabeth herself has been presented as one of them, although current understanding suggests this has been much exaggerated.

The emergence and gradual acceptance of the clergy family raised the question of where they fitted into the social order. Priests could now possess land, and many began to wheel and deal so that they had property to pass to their heirs, so clergy quickly began to look like minor gentry. The process of slowly climbing the social scale can be observed in the Archers, though by the end of the story there was a snake as well as a ladder.

The clergy wife also emerges at this time, although it is harder to find out much about them. There are seven clergy wives in this story, since two Archers married twice. Clergy wives often brought property into a marriage, adding to their new family's status. They also made it possible for clergy to have a household and offer hospitality, in the same way the gentry did. Rectories were provided with the job, and the clergy were expected to keep them in good repair. This they could do if their income was reasonable but if not, then the dilapidated rambling rectory of Foulness was the outcome. The rectory at Quainton remains as a private Queen Ann house. Finchley's C18 century rectory, I remember from my childhood, but is now demolished and replaced by flats.

Overall, the first generation of Archers was modestly comfortable; the second, in spite of the Civil War and its aftermath, improved its status; as did the next; until the fourth generation arrived at a fairly luxurious lifestyle, before snaking downhill in the final one. Whilst the first three generations had to work their way through university as servants of wealthier students, the fourth and fifth generations had become well-off enough for their families to pay for them.

The question arises as to the motivation that might lead a man to become a priest. A sense of calling and spiritual conviction has always been considered fundamental to a priestly vocation, however priesthood could simply be the easy path for any graduate who did not want to be a lawyer. The university curriculum presupposed a clerical vocation, since it was comprised of subjects designed for clerical formation.

Being a priest was relatively secure and safe. For men who were sensitive and not that ambitious, a quiet country parish provided a home to bring up a family, enough to live on, the respect of their parishioners, the satisfaction of ministering to a flock, and leisure to write poetry and prose, or socialise with like-minded clergy and gentry. Thomas senior had a brother Benjamin who spent his life in two tiny Dorset parishes, and consequently has left little story behind him.

Many priests did, like the Archers, follow in their fathers' footsteps. As sons of the rectory, they were exposed to their fathers' ministry on a daily basis and thus well able to judge their own suitability for such a calling. Familiarity can of course breed contempt; some sons would decide not to become clergy, and some would become comfortable conformists rather than passionate priests. No doubt, fathers actively encouraged their sons' calling, with the inevitable likelihood that some were pushed into it without personal conviction. There were always some who saw the church as a path to power and success in worldly terms. It would be shallow to assume such people entirely lacked faith, but more probably they saw serving the institution of the church as an expression of that faith. Patrons and preferment are words that ring throughout this period of history, but for the Archers they never meant much more than getting a parish. There are no bishops, deans, or archdeacons in the Archer story, and only one prebendary.

Since this is an account of five individual clergy, each of whom lived at a particular time in a particular milieu, our understanding of each of them must embrace the period and the circumstances in which they lived. James' and Edward's ministries were complicated by the Civil War, although being a generation apart meant that they dealt with the conflict very differently. Benjamin lived in the shadow of that war, but lived to see the coming of the House of Orange and Protestant ascendancy. Thomas grew up in the age of Walpole when sleeping dogs and dogma were left undisturbed, whereas his son could well have been a rake from a Hogarth cartoon.

Although a study of individuals, this is also a social study, since no man is an island and everybody connects. My own introduction to the Clergy Database came through attending a conference at Oxford on 17th century social relations. It was fascinating to find a group of scholars and students who were themselves being woven into a social body through the interdependence of their researches, reflecting something of the interdependent world we were studying. It seems that society is always about who you know – or, as a young friend of mine added, what you know about who you know!

We often are helped to understand others through seeing them reflected in their friends and families. So, part of the reconstructive work in the study of individual clergy must include questions and observations about their families, patrons, friends, and contacts. Sometimes the answers are immediately obvious, at other times there is a good deal of detective work to do before specific names emerge. When they do so, they can be surprising; some friendships cross norms of class, gender, and political convictions. Some patrons connect through distant family ties, whilst others seem to arise from accidental and unlikely encounters. So, the story of the Archers will include the search for their patrons and some reconstruction of their extended family links and friendships.

Location plays a key role in defining people and their experiences. The general mass of the population in these times were unlikely to move far from where they were born. The gentry and aristocracy were more mobile by virtue of the horse and, for the better off, the carriage. One or other or both of these can generally be assumed as necessary for the clergy and their ministry. Benjamin specifically bequeaths the family chaise to his wife, and Thomas the younger complains of the expense of keeping a horse.

Clergy travelled from a young age to schools or universities, and generally would own horses and carriages, or hire or borrow horses to visit friends and family. Those who served more than one church would depend on such transport to travel between their churches. As it happens, the only Archer actually to be a pluralist was the elder Thomas, whilst his son needed a horse to cover the many parishes of which he was simply a curate. His father and mother retained strong social contacts in Norfolk with family and friends, which meant frequent visits to the county. Ann Archer's parents lived in Windsor, which in part explains their carriage, although it would also have given them status and authority in the village. Clergy mobility provided them with a variety of experiences and surely gave them a greater breadth of awareness and understanding of what was going on in the country as a whole.

The study of one family does not provide a universal picture of Church of England clergy, but the hope is that it will continue a process that will lead to a broader consensus on how clergy were, and indeed are, shaped. And as other stories are researched and shared, we will be able to compare and contrast the results, and build up a fuller understanding of the English parish priest in history.

Sources

Are ubiquitous, but a helpful overview can be found in *A Thousand Years of the English Parish,* Anthea Jones, Windrush. 2000

Notes

1. *Images of Muhammed,* Tarif Khalidi, Doubleday. 2009
2. *Gentry,* Adam Nicolson, Harper Press. 2011
3. Oxford Dictionary of National Biography
4. *James Woodforde: The Diary of a Country Parson 1758–1802,* edited by John Beresford, OUP 1978
5. John Wesley became the father of Methodism, but remained a Church of England priest all his life. George Whitfield was his ordained colleague in mission. Both published journals which were designed to be published and act as apologetics for their cause.
6. *The Country Parson in English History*, A. Tindal Hart, Phoenix House. 1959
7. *Registers of ... the Foundation of Exeter College Oxford,* C.W. Boase, Oxford. 1894
8. *The Life and Times of Anthony Wood 1632–1695.* On-line or libraries.

James Archer (1588–1676):
First Generation

Sawbridgeworth, Hertfordshire, 25 August, 1588. A family gather around the 15th century font of Great St Mary's Church; the same octagonal font remains in place until this day. The church registers tell of nine Archers living in the town at this time. Eight were children baptised in that font between 1571 and 1588, one every two years, suggesting that they were all of the same parentage. But only one has a parent recorded – Grace, daughter of George. So, it is likely that he was the father of all the other children, too. George's wedding to Ann Milton took place in 1569. The last of their children was James. There are no other records of this family, suggesting that George, Ann, and their family were of a humble background.

Many inhabitants of Sawbridgeworth earned their living from the river running through their town. Shipping and trade, maltsters and brewers flourished; maybe the Archers worked by the river, too. Young James would have shared a crowded cottage and grown up familiar with the working underbelly of Sawbridgeworth life. It is stating the obvious to say that he was the only character in this study who did not grow up in a clergy household.

Their elderly minister presiding at his baptism was Nicholas Compton. He read the wordy and doctrinally-complex baptism service as laid down in the 1552 Prayer Book, and solemnly dipped the baby James in the water within the font. However, he did not preach, since he was not himself a graduate and therefore had no licence to preach – a ruling that was re-enforced in an Episcopal Visitation in 1586. The inhabitants of Sawbridgeworth seldom heard a sermon therefore, much to the frustration of many of them. Many longed for a new young presbyter, trained at one of the universities and able to excite his flock with the deeper mysteries of the faith. The new Protestant faith was only beginning to take root in the average parish church after the accession of Queen Elizabeth in 1560, and people needed much challenging to root out the "errors" of the old Catholic faith. Sawbridgeworth, like other English towns, was on the hunt for potential "godly" clergy.

The Reformation faith was still often under attack from within and without. Only a month before James' baptism, the Spanish king – on behalf of the Pope – had sent an Armada of warships to invade Britain and restore Roman Catholicism. The weather and water had seen to most of the ships, which the English tended to interpret as a sign that God was with them and their reformed faith. The family round the font would no doubt have this great deliverance in mind as they submerged their youngest in the waters of new life.

Surrounding the town were the manors of the gentry, some of whom were significant families. Although Sawbridgeworth was a small country town, its proximity to London and the court made it an ideal base for several famous families. The Boleyns had occupied Pishobury Manor since 1534, and the Seymours took over from them. It seems it was a manor to reward the relatives of Henry VIII's latest wife! In 1572, William Lord Burghley leased Says Farm as a country retreat from the burdens of court life. Then there were the Josselyns of Hyde Hall; John Josselyn being Latin Secretary to Archbishop Parker. At nearby Tednambury were the Parkers, who had added the titles of Lord Morley and Lord Monteagle to their more pedestrian family name of Parker. More humble were the Leventhorpes of Shinglehall who, like the Parkers, were originally staunch Roman Catholics. Edward Leventhorpe died on a pilgrimage to Rome in 1566, leaving a six-year-old son called John. It was this John who changed sides and became a fervent puritan gentleman, active in the town and deeply involved in Hertfordshire society.

Because we know James went to university, we equally know that he must have had an education that went beyond basic reading and writing, and encompassed Latin and even Greek. The question is, where and from whom did he obtain such an education? There is no sign of there having been a school in Sawbridgeworth. There was one in nearby Broxbourne, but there are no records before 1597. Even if he had found a basic schoolmaster, would that have prepared him for university? More likely, one of the gentry families spotted his potential, became his patron, and took care of his education.

The courtly families were unlikely to have had time to undertake schooling a local lad. The Parkers were Catholics, leaving the likely candidates as the recently converted Leventhorpes. Sir John Leventhorpe was passionate for the Reformation and the preaching of the Bible. Also, his son John was almost the same age as James, and would in all likelihood have had a tutor. Why not let the tutor teach the two of them and prepare James for a biblical ministry himself?

Like many an Elizabethan boy groomed for the ministry, James turned out to be an apt pupil and by 1602 he was on his way to Christ's College Cambridge, ready to begin a degree in classics and theology. His patron, family, and supporters in Sawbridgeworth would have no doubt helped him financially and with advice, and perhaps accompanied him to the university that was to be his home for the next eight years or so. The work would have been hard, the surroundings and company pleasant, and his horizons would have rapidly expanded. Chapel would be compulsory, morning and evening and, unlike Sawbridgeworth, sermons would have been plentiful. Initially at least, he would have acted as a servant to older boys or those who could afford to pay for their fees. The Master of Christ's, Edmund Barwell, had a reputation for being a kind and fatherly figure, giving the college a sense of family. He is said to have held radical views but the term in that period is relative. He is said to have declined becoming chancellor because it would not give him the pastoral and proselytising opportunities he had as Master.[1]

Soon after his arrival, the university buzzed with speculations following the death of the aged queen and the arrival of a new king from Scotland as her heir. Great expectations were afoot in the kingdom. The many Roman Catholic gentry and families who remained secretly, if not outwardly, loyal to the Pope, thought the Scottish king was bound to be of their opinion, especially since his mother had been Mary Queen of Scots. The puritans, on the other hand, were assured James was a learned scholar, a lover of the Bible, and respectful of the Reformation in his home country, as in England.

When the king convened a conference to discuss the religious settlement, both sides were on tip-toe. Alas, the outcome left the Catholics disaffected and the puritans pressing for greater changes yet to the Elizabethan settlement. Cambridge would surely have been full of opinions and viewpoints, and the teenaged James would have been drinking it all in, inwardly establishing his future theological and political views. He received his BA in 1604 and his MA in 1608;[2] like many a university student, he now had to make decisions about the future, although from the moment he was picked out simply for a university education there was little doubt that he would enter the ministry of the church.

At this point in the account of James' early life, we should take a moment to consider a fragmentary 18th century document purporting to have additional information about his life. In 1773, the antiquarian William Cole added some notes to his miscellany on Cambridgeshire, now in the British Library. Being manuscript notes, they remain somewhat jumbled but apparently a Mrs Chattoe had left Cole an old bursar's account book for the year 1578, relating to the fellows of Trinity College. Cole adds that "on the cover of this folio account are pasted two pieces of paper" giving details of three people named Archer, one of whom was James, and another; his son Edward. Concerning James, Cole had written in his notes of October 31, 1773:

"A member of Trinity – he used to say he was a preacher and MA in Queen Elizabeth's day. By which expression, I conceive that he meant to carry the time back as far as he possibly could and therefore the inst. came within that period c.1602. But for fear of mistake it may not be amiss to consult also the beginning of James I's reign, if there be occasion. He died about the year 1676, aged 100."[3]

As so often with new information, it raises more questions than answers. Could he be registered at Christ's and yet be a member of Trinity, where there is no record of his registration? Since his burial was in 1676, how could he have been more than 88 when he died? To be a preacher in Elizabeth's time can at best only refer to informal preaching, since he was not ordained in her reign.

Small wonder Cole tactfully qualifies the information he has received, rightly expressing the likelihood that James' actual ordination will be found in the time of James I.

James was now ready to fulfil his calling to be ordained. Cambridge being in the diocese of Ely, his bishop was Martin Heton who has been shown to have had a close relationship with his ordinands. As Kenneth Fincham has convincingly demonstrated,[4] the pastoral activities of the post-Reformation bishops were intended to embody apostolic ideals, especially those that St Paul outlined to Timothy. Heton assiduously presided over his diocesan visitations, became personally acquainted with his parochial clergy and his ordinands, and "preached often" a 17th century accolade. He ordained James as deacon on 31 May, 1607, before he had completed his MA, and priested him a year later with his MA under his belt. The priesting, on 22 May, 1608, was at the Bishop's Palace at Downham near Ely. The Bishop's register has an unusual footnote that seems to indicate a promise that James would shortly be given his own living as vicar of Soham.

"To discharge/be appointed to office of Rector of Soame ('Cura Rectoris (de Some) functurus ut per Literas Decan. El:')."[5]

Apparently, the Bishop had promised James the living of Soham when he ordained him. But Heton died in 1609, and presumably the plan fell through with his demise. For a humble graduate, obtaining a church living was not an easy task. It would depend on having the ear of a bishop, or the backing of a local patron, or the availability of a college appointment.

It was the college that now helped James when, on 29, May 1609, he was licensed as curate to the historic Round Church Cambridge, St Sepulchre's. It seems that a series of young graduate curates ran St Sepulchre's for short periods before finding a living for themselves. They could stay in Cambridge to complete their studies, supported by their colleges and friends, making the church an ideal stepping stone to a future incumbency. With so many chapels and colleges in Cambridge, it was presumably not an onerous task. Two years later another curate was licensed, so it looks as if James had a short ministry there.

With the breakdown of the arrangement to become vicar of Soham and the loss of a sympathetic bishop, what did someone like James – with his limited family connections – do next? He could stay in Cambridge, hoping to catch the eye of a patron, or return home to Sawbridgeworth where he was known and had supporters, especially the Leventhorpes. Furthermore, exciting things were happening spiritually in Sawbridgeworth, which he would have been anxious to experience for himself. And then there was the question of marriage, and where to look for a suitable bride who would be a helpmeet in his ministry.

So, by the summer of 1611, James was back in his home town again, meeting old friends and probably staying with his family, unless the Leventhorpes opened their home to him. Familiar streets of typical Elizabethan timbered homes brought back many a childhood memory – after all, he had only been 14 when he left. Meanwhile, a new vicar had arrived in Sawbridgeworth, named Abias Tuer who, like most of the new university-trained clergy, was a moderate puritan. Tuer's first name was itself a clue to his family background – Abias being a version of Obadiah, the Old Testament prophet whose passionate denunciations of evil must have embodied his parents' hopes for their son. He in turn took evil seriously, and in 1618 he was involved in a case of witchcraft, believing his brother to have been cursed. When Sir John Leventhorpe died in 1626, his will made mention of two clergy to whom he owed a debt of gratitude – one was Abias Tuer of Sawbridgeworth, and the other was Alexander Strange of neighbouring Buntingford and Layston, whose vision of a godly commonwealth spread beyond his immediate parish boundaries.

It was to Strange's parish of Layston and Buntingford that James was drawn as he returned. The previous vicar had been George Dent, who had died tragically young in 1604, but not before he had married a local lady from a merchant's family – Ellen Cherry, who gave birth to a son, Samuel, around the time of her husband's death. Alexander Strange was Dent's successor, instituted as vicar of Layston on 16 April, 1604. Strange is recorded as being a thoughtful preacher, passionately concerned for the economic and social welfare of his people as well as their spiritual lives. It so happens that Strange wrote a memoir of his own ministry, now known as the *Layston Parish Memorandum Book*, re-published in modern times as *This Little Commonwealth*[6] – a phrase he frequently used of his parish, encapsulating the puritan vision of the parish as an outpost of the kingdom of God amidst a sea of secular godlessness.

Having come to Layston in 1604, Strange "for 46 years was taken up with instructing the people and mediating peace between quarrellers, and amongst other good works, caused the establishment of this house of God".

So reads his epitaph, inscribed on a tablet in St Peter's, Buntingford, where Strange had his new church built nearer the centre of the local population. His memorial there depicts him in the pulpit, with a Bible in one hand and an hourglass in the other. Yet, according to his memorandum book, much of his time was spent on those other activities spoken of in his epitaph. In particular, he was constantly engaged in the vexed issue of how to help the poor. His vision was to make his parish a loving and caring one in which the deserving poor were generously cared for. But then he found that people moved into the parish because of the benefits available; a bit like people today move to get their children into a good church school! Furthermore, some of the better-off people saw a chance to make money by buying up property in the parish to let out to the poor who wanted to move in! So, Strange had to challenge the poor and the rich as he strove to establish his model community.

He worked closely in conjunction with the magistrates, including Sir John Leventhorpe, preaching his vision, which they as godly laity must help bring to pass. To help him bring about this vision, he had the support of two significant puritan landowners – the Crouches of Layston, and the Leventhorpes of Sawbridgeworth. It is recognised that the years 1570 to 1640 saw an upsurge in the business of church courts. Puritanism may have proclaimed the gospel of faith alone, but it also concluded that strict adherence to a moral code showed people that they had need of salvation as well as calling them to bear the fruits of that salvation. And what better than being hauled before the courts to show a man his need of repentance!

Alexander Strange was a Cambridge graduate like James, but his background was clearly wealthier. He was rector of at least two other Hertfordshire churches as well as Layston, and he had connections with London and local gentry who contributed generously to his projects. He also had land and income of his own, which he poured into his project. He never married, focusing fully on his parish visions. James would have watched and noted how Strange fulfilled his calling, and his observations would place him in good stead once he had a parish of his own. But before that was to come about, he himself was in need of a godly wife. And it was at Layston that he met Ellen Dent – the widow of Strange's predecessor who had died in 1604 – and her seven-year-old son, Samuel. Her family were local, the Cherrys of Great Munden and Cherry Green. The chemistry happened, and they were married on New Year's Day [25 March] 1612 at St Botolph's church in the City of London,[7] where Ellen's father had business interests. Their marriage licence describes James simply as a clerk of Sawbridgeworth and Ellen as a widow of Buntingford.

Now with a wife and stepson to support, James could no longer delay his search for a parish. Many gentry possessed an advowson, the right of appointment to a church, but it could be years before their advowson became free. James could only turn to his childhood patron and friend Sir John Leventhorpe. But there were no openings available at the time. However, he had many relatives, including the Parker Morleys who remained a convinced Catholic family. There was a vacant parish, of which they were the patrons, that they were able to offer James as a family favour; Yardley, now in modern-day Birmingham. Making this connection became possible when I studied the memorials that remain in St Mary's Sawbridgeworth, especially that of Sir John Leventhorpe:

HERE LYETH THE BODIES OF SIR JOHN LEVENTHORP,
KNT., AND BARONETT, SONNE AND HEIRE OF EDWARD
LEVENTHORPE, ESQUIRE, WHO DIED IN HIS TRAVELLS, AND
LYETH BURIED AT ROME; AND OF MARY, THE DAUGHTER
OF SIR HENRY PARKER, KNT. SONNE AND HEIRE APPARENT
UNTO THE RIGHTE HONORABLE THE LORD MORLEY, WHOE
TOOKE TO WIFE JOAN, THE ELDEST DAUGHTER OF SIR JOHN
BROGRAVE, KNT. ATTORNEY OF THE DUTCHY OF LANCASTER,
BY WHOME HE HAD SIXE SONNES AND EIGHTE DAUGHTERS,
AND AFTER HE HAD DONN HIS COUNTRY GOOD AND FAITH-
FULL SERVICE BOTH IN PEACE AND WARRE, AS WELL
ABROADE AS AT HOME, BY THE SPACE OF ALMOST FOURTY
YEARES, AND HAVING WITH GOOD COMMENDATION PAST
THROUGH THE EMYNENT PLACES OF THE COUNTRY, AND
DURING THE WHOLE COURSE OF HIS PILGRIMAGE HERE ON
EARTH HAVING LIVED IN THE FEARE OF GOD, HE DYED,
IN THE FAITH OF JESUS CHRIST THE 23RD OF SEPTEMBER,
ANNO DOM. 1625, LEAVING BEHINDE HIM ALIVE FOUR
SONNES AND SEAVEN DAUGHTERS.

So, here we read of Edward Leventhorpe, who was a Catholic who died on pilgrimage to Rome, where he is buried, and his wife Mary Parker – both members of local wealthy Roman Catholic land-owning families – whose son John Leventhorpe had become a puritan. Mary Parker's brother was Sir William Parker, Fourth Baron Monteagle, and Lord Morley's and Sir John Leventhorpe's uncle. The Parkers had land in various places apart from Hertfordshire, including Yardley, Worcester, and its advowson, the parish church of St Edburgha. Although Parker had technically professed allegiance to the Church of England after his close shave with the law from his connection with the Gunpowder Plot, most people believed he retained his Catholic loyalties to the end of his life. Either way, he was prepared to give James his break as the authorised incumbent of Yardley.

James' appointment would also depend upon the Bishop of Worcester, Henry Parry – a chaplain to Queen Elizabeth, who attended her at her deathbed. He had also been a friend of Richard Hooker, the leading apologist for the reformed Church of England. James met Parry in his palace at Worcester on 30 December, and was found to be an acceptable candidate for Yardley. He made the necessary oaths of allegiance to the monarch and the bishop, and prepared himself for his institution and licensing at St Edburgha's on 14 January, 1613.[8] St Edburgha's was a 13th century church named after a granddaughter of Alfred the Great, reminding people of how ancient the English church was. Within the churchyard was, and is still, a classic Elizabethan half-timbered schoolhouse that James would have been responsible for. Birmingham may have spilt all around the ancient churchyard, church, and schoolhouse, but within the churchyard itself little has changed.

The rectory now became the family home for the next 64 years. Starting with just James, Ellen, and 10-year-old Samuel, the family steadily expanded, though it remained a small family by 17th century standards.

From the parish registers:

Edward – baptised 23 January, 1614
Blanche – baptised 26 January, 1616/7; but buried four months later
    on 16 May
Francis – baptised 17 October, 1619
Ann – baptised in 1621
Ailmer – baptised 5 September, 1624.
"An infant of Mr James Archer" was baptised and buried 9 April,
    1627

These names do not follow the standard 17th century practice of naming children after their parents and grandparents. Edward could be from the Leventhorpes and Ann could be after her grandmother, but both are common names. Ailmer is named after a leading Yardley family, and almost certainly an Aylmer was one of his godparents. Was this a deliberate protest against following convention and an expression of Christian liberty? It was certainly unusual that none of the children carried their parents' names.

James kept impeccable records, and the page from the registers that includes Edward's baptism is an example of his care and neat mind; handwriting is perhaps the next best thing to a portrait in evaluating someone's character.

There were no more children after the infant death of 1627. Maybe Ellen came close to death herself and they decided on not risking her life again; maybe she was anyhow past childbearing age at 44. She died in 1643, aged about 60, leaving James a widower for more than 30 years.

Samuel Dent married and stayed in Yardley, so in 1629 Ellen became a grandmother and James a step-grandfather to a child named after himself, James Dent.

Of all Ellen's and James' children, only one, Edward, has left any mark in history since he followed in his father's footsteps in becoming a minister, establishing the second generation of post-Reformation Archer clergy. His story will be a separate one, but obviously there were implications for James in bringing up a son who was destined for ministry. How much was Edward's choice and how much his father's grooming? Why did none of the other sons follow this path? Was money an issue, since it could be costly putting a son through university? In fact, Edward was a sizar, working his way through college just as his father had. Was it a matter of intelligence or calling?

Meanwhile, James had work to do to earn his living. He was to spend 64 years in Yardley, much of which was to be spent in the everyday work of a clergyman, leading worship, preaching and teaching, baptising, marrying and burying, visiting and listening, and dispensing wise advice. With the lessons of Strange's Little Commonwealth firmly in his mind, he set out to stamp out the destructive behaviour of some of his parishioners. And one man, Adams, seemed to be the focus of his determination to see that the unruly and ungodly were brought to book. It may have taken a year or two to carry his parishioners with him, but in 1616 James takes the lead in signing a petition to the Worcester Quarter Sessions, preserved as *a petition from the parishioners of Yardley*.[9]

"We whose names are here written do further signifie that the named Addams is a common and a notorious drunkard. Item he is a notorious swearer and blasphemer of God and a prophaner of the Sabbath. Item he is a contemner and railer against the minister. Item he has been excommunicated ten or twelve years for divers adulterous acts and for anything we know so continues… Item he hath sold ale without a recognizance. Item he beat his wife most cruellie that she was all bloodie. Item the same Addams being drunk in Droitwich wished he might meet somebody to fall out with that he might kill them and be hanged out of the way. Item he is a common miscaller of his neighbours and abuser of them" signed by James Archer, Minister and 12 others. 26.1.1616."

Parish finances also called for his attention. All must be done decently and in order to glorify God, down to the last detail, which is reflected in his impeccable parish registers – a model of clarity and order. On 15 August, 1616, he and his leading laymen set out the basis of how the vicar's income from tithes was evaluated. Some of the tithes belonged to the lay rector, so that there must have been ample room for disputes. James and his wardens set themselves to make things clear:

> "Item, there dothe appear and belonge unto the said Vicar of Yardeley, aforesayde, all and all manner of Teythes, and Tennethes, of all manner of Cattelles, and of fruits, and all and all manner of Oblacions and Offerings, Obventions, Profits, Churche or Spirituall dueties, herbage, mortuaries, and all small tyths, arysinge, happeninge, fallinge, or cominge within the sayde Parish of Yardley, and there usually payde to the Vicar there (Excepting, the tythes or tennthes of all corne and grayne, and of haye within the said Parish) doe also appertayne and belonge to the sayde Vicar and Vicarage of Yardeley, which said tythes and tennethes of corne and grayne and of haye, within the said parish, does appertayne and belong to, and have been usually paid to the Parsons or Propriertaires, and their farmers, of the Parsonage of Yardley aforesayde:
>
> James Archer, minister;
> Thomas Dolphin and John Blund, Churchwardens; Edward Swift
> and John Hopkins, Sydesmen."[10]

Another small window into a vicar's modest financial reward comes from the mention of the monies he was paid for preaching at the funerals of his wealthier laity. For example, in 1616 Henry Devereux left him 40sh. for preaching his funeral sermon, and entrusted him with distributing his final bequests to the poor. There were to be many such bequests and requests in his lifetime. Indeed, James' ministry is chiefly reflected in the accounts of the leading gentry in his parish, for these were largely the people whose records have been preserved. The lesser laity get mentioned only for misdemeanours, like the miscreant Addams. So, an account of some of those families will present James in context and describe something of a clergyman's role in society at this time, but we must remember that his work with the poor and working families will not have left us with historic records.[11]

The Folliotts lived in Blakesley Hall. At the beginning of James' ministry, the head of this family was Aylmer. This was the name of James' younger son, suggesting that Aylmer Folliott was godfather to Ailmer Archer. In 1638, the Folliotts contributed three additional bells to St Edburgha's, inscribed:

> "The Bequest of Aylmer Folliott Esquire, 1638; H.I.S. Nazarenus (sic), Rex Judaeorum, Fili Dei, Miserere Mei, 1638; Humphrey Hobday, and Richard Bissell, Churchwardens 1638."

This may well have been a response to Archbishop Laud's directives about restoring the dignity of the parish church. When Aylmer Folliott died, he bequeathed to his vicar his best hat! There is a certain intimacy about wearing a dead man's hat, but also the Folliotts were probably of a similar financial standing to the Archers and recognised that a good hat was not to be sneezed at.

More challenging were the somewhat wild and unpredictable Ests. The original Thomas Est had risen in society as Gentleman of the Bedchamber to Henrys V and VI, but although a streak of tempestuosity ran through the family, it was increasingly restrained by their growing puritanism. Edward Est's gift of a new pulpit to Yardley church in 1627 indicates that they were backing the puritan emphasis on preaching, and encouraging the parson to provoke his people to love and good works by his preaching. Edward Est's name has recently been rediscovered on a front panel of the pulpit, beneath the varnish. The pulpit was provocatively placed in front of the communion table, and only moved to its present position in the 19th century.

There were several Edward Ests over the years. One died in 1625, and James Archer would have taken his funeral. His memorial describes him as:

"That religious gentleman...outer barrister of ye Inner Temple, who peacibly and cheerfully exchanged this mortall life for immortalitie and glorie with his Redeemer when he was about the age of 27 yeares. The time of his pilgrimage was not longe, but in that he lived well he fulfilled many dayes.
His life was short, but the sooner he had rest, God takes them youngest whom he loves best."
Even more poignant, perhaps, is the memorial to an Edward born in 1633:
"In his childhood, being deprived of the sense of seeing, he made that happy use of so severe a calamity as not to admit those vanities into his mind and actions which he was therefore disabled from beholding with his eyes. And therefore he wisely turned his thoughts from beholding the concerns and enjoyments of this life to contemplate and study the joys of a better, and spent his time in profitable meditations, pious ejaculations, affectionate soliloquies, singing of psalms and other holy exercises of a Christian devotion."

He reputedly learned the whole Bible by heart, as well as other godly and useful books, and died a bachelor in the 70th year of his age.

But in contrast to these two pious puritan Ests, the rest of the family followed their more unruly past. In 1631, two Est brothers were involved in instigating a riot in Yardley, and soon found themselves before the Worcester Quarter Sessions. The 1636 Quarter Sessions record the case of Thomas Est assaulting Humphrey Greswolde and John Flynt, constable of Yardley.[12] Yet later on, Thomas Est showed his respect for his vicar when he made James an executor of his will in 1655, and left him 10 shillings for a funeral sermon.

The Folliotts and the Ests were the main puritan families who sided with Parliament in the Civil War, unlike the Dods of Lea Hall, who were firm royalists. On the eve of the Civil War in 1637, "certayne differences fell out" between Charles Dod and Thomas Est on account of Est's "disgraceful words against ye Coate of Armes of ye sayd Charles Dod". The Dods went on to keep a low profile during the war, during which Charles Dod was fined £30 and required to take the engagement (an oath made in support of Parliament to demonstrate his acceptance of the Commonwealth). The Restoration parliament appointed Robert Dod as a lieutenant by a printed commission, dated 20 April, 1660. Charles Dod had Roman Catholic leanings. His will was not only pious, but generous to the poor of Yardley. There remain a number of Dod memorials in Yardley church, and by the time of James Archer's death, Robert Dod had become the patron of St Edburgha's. As for the original conflict between the Ests and Dods, it was happily recorded that peace between them was restored by the mediation of James Archer.[13]

The Greswoldes of Hall Green, being the oldest and wealthiest family in Yardley, were supportive of the king. In 1637, Humphrey Greswolde paid for the new altar rails for the church. As a royalist, he would have been more inclined to accept the injunctions for dignifying the church recently issued by Archbishop Laud. Unfortunately, we have no way of knowing whether James was happy or unhappy with this addition to the church, but he clearly went along with it. The puritans saw this Laudian injunction as yet another move away from biblical simplicity, back to the ceremonial that had befogged the gospel prior to the Reformation. It seems this would have been the view of James' son Edward, but the new rails suggest that James was more moderate, and perhaps reflect his own love of order. The same year, Humphrey Greswolde – in accordance with his duty as lay rector to keep the chancel in good repair – joined with the churchwardens William Acock and William Bissell in having the chancel "ceiled".

In spite of his royalist sympathies, in 1630 Humphrey Greswolde was shrewd enough to turn down a knighthood, for which he was fined £12, since selling off knighthoods was one of Charles I's stratagems for raising money after he finally decided to reign without parliament from 1629. Paradoxically, at the height of the Commonwealth in 1658, Humphrey is once again fined by the State; this time for refusing militia duty under the Commonwealth.[14] Nevertheless, the next year he became constable of Yardley – another carefully calculated compromise, freeing him from militia duty, but nevertheless he still accepted a local role under the auspices of the parliamentary regime.

When he died in 1671, out of the rectory and greater tithes, he left £5 per annum to pay for four gowns for four poor and aged men, one from each quarter of the parish. There is a certain puritan tidiness about this bequest, but in fact it followed the pattern of gentry wills prior to the Reformation. James Archer would have been with him, preparing him for death, maybe advising on his charitable bequests, and would have taken the funeral. There are several Greswolde monuments in the church today, including that of Humphrey.

The Acocks of Acocks Green became a Roundhead family and fought in the Civil War. It was William Acock who contributed to the new church ceiling, and was one of St Edburgha's influential churchwardens.

Job Marston of Hall Green, in his will of 1654, left 10 shillings to the minister who preached his funeral sermon [James Archer], and asked that his son be brought up in the fear of the Lord and schooled accordingly. The Marstons were another ancient family who manifested a concern for the care of the poor. A few years later, a charity was set up by another Job Marston, which still operates in Yardley to this day.

Keeping the peace between ambitious and proud gentry families was a task James seems to have managed, to his credit. The task grew more onerous as the Civil War approached, when everyone was walking on a knife-edge and families lined up on opposing sides. James himself had to choose a pathway through the uncertainties of those days. His son Edward had taken the presbyterian direction, and when war broke out he took his family to London, leaving behind the opportunity of becoming vicar of Enville, which living James had previously bought the right of appointment from John and Abigail Whorwood for £40.[15] James was too old for such a dramatic course even if he believed in the presbyterian cause, which he may or may not have done. However, Edward named his first son after his father, suggesting that a cordial family link remained.

The great gentry families dominated the life of Yardley in James' time. He accepted the social order and used these gentry to forward his original vision of a godly commonwealth. But the vision was overshadowed by the gathering storm clouds of the Civil War. As we saw, he was able to bring two opposing families together in 1637, and his ministry was now channelled into one of reconciliation within the yawning political divide. The greatest threat to his harmonious vision, his little commonwealth, would undoubtedly have been the war. For all his concern to settle disputes and preside over a godly parish, neither the vicar nor anyone else could bring peace to an increasingly divided and restive nation. James was approaching 50 when the violence finally flared up. One would imagine he found it all disturbing and distressing. The Civil War raged in the Midlands, and in 1643 reached Yardley's doorstep when Prince Rupert sacked puritan Birmingham. Today there are still deep grooves in the exterior wall of St Edburgha's Church attributed to soldiers sharpening their weapons there during the war. The burial records include an unknown soldier, a victim of one of the nearby battles no doubt, who had stumbled as far as Yardley before dying.

The war disturbed the smooth running of society, as menfolk went off to fight and opposing armies ravished the countryside. The economic consequences were dire, and incomes from farming fell or dried up. The consequence for clergy would have been the loss of their tithes. From the beginning of the war, Parliament addressed this issue by vetting the worthy clergy who were deemed to be godly preachers and making them grants in lieu of lost tithes. In September 1649, James was granted by Parliament an Augmentation of Stipend, ordered by the Plundered Ministers Committee, from sale of dean and chapter lands. And again in 1651, the Trustees for the Maintenance of Preaching Ministers give an Augmentation from the revenue of the Dean and Chapter of Worcester.[16]

It looks like James' income was sufficient to make a personal gift to the church, in the shape of a fourth bell in 1653 inscribed, "all praise and glori bee to god for ever, 1653 JA". This was surely a statement of hope for the future of the parish church, whatever the uncertainties of the political and ecclesiastical shape of things to come.

James must have been puritan enough, yet pragmatic enough, to ride the storms of civil war and republicanism to emerge still in his parish after the Restoration. He seems to have held his tongue during the Interregnum and concentrated on the practicalities of parish life and the physical and spiritual welfare of his people. As a result, he was spoken well of and gave no cause to be removed in 1662, since he would have meekly, and perhaps happily, accepted the new settlement.

But the same was not true of his son Edward, who was ejected in 1662. The records do not give us the information that we would dearly love to have, so we do not know what the relationship between father and son was like; was it respect or disagreement? But how much did they see of one another, since Edward was many miles away from his ageing father? How well did James ever know his grandchildren? And what was his reaction to Edward's death in 1672? Answers to these questions would help us assess the legacy of the Civil War on clergy family life, but we will have to look to pointers elsewhere.

There is very little evidence from Yardley about the final phase of James' ministry. He was a widower for the last 30 years of his ministry there. With the publication of the 1662 Prayer Book, parish life reverted to a more ordered style and services and sacraments continued to be ministered. With no clergy retirement available, he remained in post to the end of his long life.

James Archer was buried at St Edburgha's, Yardley, on 18 May, 1675, aged 88 years. He could look back on the good old days of Queen Elizabeth, and to the puritan gentry who talent-spotted him as a potential minister of the gospel. He was fast-tracked to Cambridge University where, in his heady days as a young man, he was moulded by his puritan teachers, albeit mostly at the moderate end of the spectrum. Set up by the bishop for a parish, the latter's death created a hiatus in those plans, leading him to return to his native Sawbridgeworth. Here he had the opportunity of seeing how the godly clergy and gentry combined to create a foretaste of God's kingdom in Hertfordshire. Again, this was a moderate model, unlike some of the millennial aberrations of extremists.

James chose his wife from this community and was ready for a parish of his own, which was brought about through the Parker relatives of the Leventhorpes. So far as we can see, he took this pattern of ministry with him from Sawbridgeworth to Yardley and stayed true to it all his life. He built strong relationships with the local gentry and acted firmly in the face of unsociable behaviour. He guided his eldest son into ministry, even buying an advowson for his future.

Edward, however, threw in his lot with the presbyterian revolution and headed for London, leaving his father uncertain how to respond to the changes introduced under Archbishop Laud. Nevertheless, James was shortly accepting Parliamentary augmentations following the loss of tithes through civil war. He may well have taken the engagement, and almost certainly used the Presbyterian Directory when the Prayer Book was proscribed. With the Civil War swirling all around him, he stayed steady in his parish and took little or no part in the conflicting views around him. As a result, he was able to retain his parish, accept the Restoration and the Act of Uniformity, and continue his vision from 1662 until his death 14 years later. Perhaps he became more muddled, spoke of being nearly 100,[3] lived as much in Elizabethan times as the present. Faithful, steady, old, and grieving the death of his son, his ministry faded into history, awaiting – like him – a future resurrection.

Sources

1. A History of the University of Cambridge, Vol 2.
2. Venn's *Alumni Cantabrigienses*, 1922; Peile's *Register of Christ's College Cambridge*, 1913.
3. William Cole's *Cambridgeshire*, 1773 Add. Mss 5845.350, British Library.
4. *Bishops and Power in Early Modern England*, Marcus K Harmes. 2013, Google Books.
5. Ordination and appointment records from the online clergy database: (CECD) CUL, EDR G/2/20 Ely Register of Licences.
6. *'This little commonwealth': Layston Parish Memorandum Book,* Hertfordshire Record Society. 2003.
7. Allegations for Marriage Licences issued by the Bishop of London ed. G J Armytage (Harleian Society).
8. Presentation Papers for Yardley, from Worcester Diocesan archives (732.4).
9. Worcestershire County Records, Calendar of the Quarter Sessions Papers 1591–1643.
10. Church Terrier of 15 August, 1616, reproduced in *Yardley and its Parish Church*, an old guidebook held in the Genealogical Society.
11. There are a number of sources for Yardley families, especially *Political and Administrative History: Political History to 1832, A History of the County of Warwick*: Volume 7: The City of Birmingham (1964), pp 270–297; *Victoria County History* for

Worcester; various Yardley Wills in which James is named: WRO[CR 299/532/1-11 Warwick CR] re Greswolde

12. Worcester Quarter Sessions 1/1/62/74 re the dispute between the Ests and the Greswoldes.

13. Web page for Acocks Green History Society. Hay Hall, by K H Sprayson, 1978.

14. State Papers

15. Pair of final Concords 1637, (Shropshire RO 2922/11/10/4/1–2).

16. Commonwealth Records: *Shaw's History of the Church*, p548, Lambeth Ms.1105a.

Edward Archer (1613–1672): Second Generation

Though James's story had a number of twists and turns to begin with, it was overall a settled life centred on only three places. By contrast, Edward's life was far more unsettled, and he lived in eight different places in his lifetime. In part, this can be attributed to the Civil War, which dominated his ministry. Edward's restless journeying from place to place, blown by the winds of change howling around the English Church, is in itself a reflection of society as a whole. Each of those locations provides a new angle on Edward and his ministry, as well as a pleasant itinerary for the modern-day researcher.

Edward was born at Yardley, Worcester, the eldest son of James and Ellen Archer. He was baptised by his father at St Edburgha's on 23 January, 1613/14. Unusually, his name does not appear to be a family name. Neither did he have close family around him, since these were all in Hertfordshire. Unlike his father, Edward was to be nurtured and educated in a clergy household. Church services and Bible readings would have been at the core of family life. Yet neither his two brothers, nor his stepbrother, followed the clerical pathway.

His father was equipped to educate his own son but there was also an Elizabethan school in the parish. Indeed, the splendid, timbered building stands to this day in the churchyard of St Edburgha's, amidst the sea of post-war Birmingham as it has spread around this medieval enclave. Edward would not have been so dependent on a patron in the way that his father had been; indeed, James himself prepared to be Edward's patron. Incidentally, Edward would be one of the first generation to have been brought up on the King James Bible of 1611.

Like any acute child, Edward must have taken on board overheard adult conversations. He would have become aware in his earliest teens that King Charles I was causing national upset by refusing to call Parliament; also that the king had married a Roman Catholic, and consequently was suspected of having Catholic sympathies himself. But however much his father and the puritans may have been frustrated by this, they still accepted God's providence and remained loyal to the ruler whom they believed they had been called to honour. This conviction they passed on to Edward.

The same bit of paper that Cole puzzled over, trying to work out what exactly happened to James Archer, also mentioned his son Edward. Cole summarised what he had read:

"Edward Archer AM was a member of Trinity College and born about 1613. So that I suppose him to have taken his Master's Degree at 7 yrs standing and that he did not come remarkably young or old to the University and in all likelihood he conveyed his MA about the age of 24 or 25 which must be about the year 1637 or 8. However it may perhaps be requisite to take in a few years before or after that."

In later years, Venn's collection of college records confirmed most of what Cole had presumed. Edward had matriculated at Trinity College in 1629 and worked his way through college as a sizar, following in his father's footsteps. He took his BA in 1633 and migrated to King's for his MA, which he was awarded in 1637. Like all Cambridge students, he would meet a variety of opinions, learn to dispute and argue his viewpoints, and make a number of friends who would stand him in good stead in the future.

Meanwhile, Edward had got himself ordained and was given oversight of a parish. Both happenings were not straightforward. In the first place, no record of the ordination has come to light, although there is no doubt that he was episcopally ordained. The question was raised in 1664 when a court was taking depositions in relation to a contested tithe case. A labourer named Daniel affirmed that Edward had told him he had been ordained by the Bishop of Coventry and Lichfield some 35 years back, about 1629.

Daniel's recollections certainly reflect an exceptionally youthful ordination. Landor,[1] in his *Staffordshire Incumbents and Parochial Records 1530-1680,* says that Edward Archer became curate of Enville, Staffs in 1632. This was a year before his BA, when he was aged only 19, far below the canonical age of 23. Given that this was the case, he would certainly have been ordained by Bishop Thomas Morton of Coventry and Lichfield. Morton was a patron of reformed theologians, a friend of Hooker, corresponded with Laud, and favoured the pan-protestant international vision of John Drury. He also had a reputation for ordaining men below the canonical age, making Edward's early ordination more likely.

The most probable scenario is that Morton had met Edward and fast-tracked him for ordination because he noted that he was learned and godly, in the parlance of the day. The ordination records for Morton's time remain, but those for his final year in Coventry have become illegible. We can only presume that Edward was indeed ordained by Morton and that he was one of those illegible entries for 1631/2.

Morton may also have seen Edward as the solution to a knotty pastoral problem. The rector of Enville in Staffordshire was Anthony Fowke MA of Queens, Oxon, who by 1618 had been classed as a lunatic. There was also a curate, John Evans, who practised magical arts in the neighbourhood and was also declared to be a lunatic in 1628! The Groby family of Enville, who were the lords of the manor, were a puritan family by this time. The wife of Ambrose Grey, Lord of Enville, attended puritan lectures in neighbouring parishes,[2] and Henry Grey, First Earl of Stamford – known as Lord Grey of Groby – was a nobleman, military leader, and staunch parliamentarian. He was also a Cambridge graduate himself, who had been a member of Trinity College in 1615. He became a moderate Presbyterian, although his second son, Thomas, turned out to be an Independent and a regicide. Maybe the Greys were putting pressure on the bishop to provide Enville with a sane and godly ministry, and Morton thought that a young and enthusiastic curate from Trinity Cambridge would sort the problem out. However, what was not sorted out seems to have been the finances of the arrangement, since Bishop Morton was translated to Durham almost immediately after appointing Edward to this tangled task. Perhaps this is why Edward wrote directly to the recently appointed archbishop, William Laud.[3]

"Petition of Edward Archer, clerk MA to Archbishop Laud. Anthony Fowke is incumbent of Enfield (sic) co. Staffs, yearly value of 8 score £'s and in Hilary term last he was begged for a lunatic having been so for 5 yrs. And the petitioner was near upon a year since appointed by his Diocesan to officiate the cure there, but as yet has received nothing for his pains… prays for the coadjutarship with an assignment of competent means out of the Rectory."

The petition is undated, but since Edward was then an MA, it must have been sometime after 1637 when his degree was recognised by King's College. The MA seemed to trigger several organisational responses. Firstly, his father concluded a deal whereby he purchased the right to appoint the next minister to St Mary's, Enville, thereby potentially setting up Edward to be the next rector. Then, on 8 August, Edward was freshly licensed as curate of Enville by Robert Wright, the new Bishop of Coventry and Lichfield. This also looks like the time that he began to make plans to marry, and 1638 is the likely date for his wedding, although Edward's is one of two Archer marriages that cannot be traced. We know nothing of his wife Mary, other than her Christian name and the will she made before her death in 1686.

This was also the time that national events were escalating towards civil war. In 1639, King Charles tried to impose the English Prayer Book on Scotland, and the first round of fighting broke out there. There is little doubt that Edward would have sympathised with the Scots, upon whom Charles sought to impose what the puritans saw as a high church, if not Roman Catholic settlement. Wars require cash, and cash came at the behest of Parliament. When convened, the Parliament was pro-puritan and angry with the king and his increasingly anti-puritan edicts. In 1639, Ithiel Smart – the vicar of Wombourne, Staffs – was cited for proclaiming a fast in direct contravention of the king's recent proclamation.[4] Since Wombourne is close to Enville , it is not surprising to find that Edward and Ithiel became friends, and there is every likelihood that Edward joined in this illegal fast for the state of the kingdom.

At that point, Anthony Fowke, the lunatic rector of Enville, died. This was when James' scheming should have come to fruition and he would have appointed Edward as Fowke's successor, but it was not to be so. Perhaps father and son were pulling in different directions over the current political crisis in church and State. And maybe Edward was beginning to see his future in a very different way. Certainly, the writing was now on the wall for the bishops, and in 1640 the Long Parliament received petitions for the abolition of "Episcopacy, Root and Branch".

Furthermore, Edward had a growing family to consider. Their first child, a daughter, is recorded in the Enville registers on 18 February, 1640/1, *Mary, dt. of Edward & Mary*: they were being traditional in their naming pattern. We know from other sources that there was to be a James and an Edward, even though a record of their baptisms is no longer extant.

Edward was a passionate man and trod where angels feared. He had been ordained early, taking on a complex parish situation, and now he threw himself into the presbyterian revolution that Parliament was rolling out from its epicentre in London, undergirded by the Westminster Assembly which, established as a committee of Parliament, began to take on the bishops' roles, including putting ministers forward for appointments. Edward probably knew and admired members of the assembly and wanted to be part of this exciting new presbyterian scene spreading out from London. The assembly appointed him to St Ethelburga's in June 1643,[5] just two months after his friend Ithiel Smart had been appointed to St Magdalene, Old Fish Street. Perhaps the two friends travelled to the capital together. They were now at the heart of the presbyterian experiment in the heart of the English church. However, the honeymoon period did not last long.

In that September, a prisoner was brought to London from Staffordshire. Francis Pitt was known to both Smart and Archer as a godly man and something of a preacher. He was a yeoman farmer who happened to rent his land from a royalist soldier, Captain Levinson. It seems that from his base in Dudley Castle, Levinson tried to purchase the parliamentary stronghold of Rushall Hall from Captain Tuthill who was in charge there. Levinson employed Francis Pitt as the go-between, along with a Jesuit priest. He promised Pitt seven years' relief from his rent if Pitt agreed, which he did. When the authorities found out about the deal, Pitt was arrested and taken to London for trial.

Smart and Archer, with two other ministers from Staffordshire, immediately visited Pitt to exhort him to repent of his "treachery", which he readily did. On 8 October, Pitt appeared before the War Council at the Guildhall, where he was tried and condemned to death. The ministers now spent hours with him and accompanied him to the gallows the following Saturday. Here, Pitt launched into a full-scale sermon, admitting his own hypocrisy and cataloguing his sins by working through the Ten Commandments and their inner application as well as outward. He accepted his imminent departure and was inwardly assured he would go to heaven.

Smart urged him to go into detail about his act of treachery. Here, Pitt began to depart from the script! Whilst he admitted his treachery, he did make sure the crowd knew it was his landlord who persuaded him to be a messenger for him. It was not easy for someone to refuse their landlord or betters, and the Civil War had confused these ancient loyalties. Pitt asked that the Council should go after the big fish because he was only a little fish. Obliquely, Pitt pointed to the captain of Rushall, even though he professed to have forgotten his name. Everyone knew it was Tuthill. Pitt also declared that the behaviour at Rushall had confused him. Drunkenness, swearing, and profanity abounded. Indeed, he had wondered whether he could really be in a parliamentary establishment at all!

Pitt also had a dig at the ministers, saying that there were so few godly ministers left in Staffordshire it was not surprising that ordinary folk like him lacked support and got led astray. Having made his points, he returned to being a conventional puritan preacher, exhorting the crowd to observe tomorrow's sabbath and live godly lives. Now Francis led the crowd in prayer. He included prayers for the king:

> "The Lord blesse the King, and I desire every honest man
> to honour him… and to obey him in what they may…
> I desire the Lord to bring him home to his Parliament, and
> to remove from him all evil counsellors… I am persuaded
> the King is an honest man though he is misled."

At this date, there was nothing treacherous in these words, but already some of the parliamentary propagandists were beginning to think differently. Pitt then retired with the ministers to pray, which he did for about half an hour. Finally, he stepped out to the gallows, and Edward Archer asked him to give a signal to tell him that as he was dying he was experiencing God's grace and mercy. This Pitt duly did, according to Edward, by beating his hands on his chest as he was asphyxiated! But this request tells us some more about Edward, namely that he was looking for spiritual signs and experiential behaviour. He was no mere academic puritan.

Edward must have pondered long and hard on this experience. Was the godly revolution really all that he had believed it to be? Was he in the right place, surrounded by the buzz of Presbyterian London, along with so many of his contemporaries? Might he be more useful back in a country parish, rather than one amongst dozens of London preaching churches? And what about the king? In London, the hostility was rising, but Francis Pitt had eloquently expressed the popular view that they had no wish to see any harm befall their anointed sovereign. Could Edward see the writing on the wall? Was he convicted by Francis Pitt's honest words?

Many pamphlets were circulating from London at this time – there was undoubtedly money to be made from the more lurid versions especially. Archer did not hurry into gratifying this appetite for pamphlets, but when he read suspect versions of Pitt's demise he and Smart decided to go into print themselves, telling their own story, from which I have taken the above account. Their definitive publication was:

> "A more exact and perfect relation of the treachery of Francis Pitt aged 65, for trying to betray Rushall Hall, Staffs to the enemy."[6]

Within a year, Edward Archer was released by Parliament from his London ministry and appointed to the parish of Leamington near Warwick. The new appointment is recorded in *The Plundered Ministers Committee Minute book 1645–7*:[7]

> "Vicar of Leamington, Warws 27th May 1645 'Edward Archer Master of Artes, a godly and orthodox divine' Replaces Thomas Lowood."

One explanation of this move by Edward is to be nearer his father in Yardley. Edward's mother had died in 1643, about the time of his move to London, which may well have further unsettled him and prompted him to ask Parliament for a move closer to his father in his bereavement. Meanwhile, restless times continued, with civil war intensifying between Parliament and the king in spite of a nominal lull after the Peace of Oxford in June 1646.

So why might Edward have uprooted his family once more a couple of years later, when he was appointed rector of Somerton? I have not found a record of that appointment, but because of Edward's clash with the authorities we know about his time there. The fact that the previous minister, Thomas Walden (or Walker), had recently been removed from his benefice precipitated the need for a new minister. Perhaps it was the growing cost of bringing up his family that led to Edward seeking a more lucrative benefice, for Somerton was a parish with an above-average income. Furthermore, it boasted a smart new vicarage built by the future Archbishop William Juxon, who had been rector of Somerton before the war. Alas, the church registers cease in 1647. They may well have been destroyed by a zealous incumbent after the Restoration, but it means that we cannot learn anything about Edward's incumbency from them.

Ironically, Somerton was a stronghold of recusants – families who remained loyal to the Roman Catholic Church and placed themselves under the jurisdiction of a Catholic priest whom they would have helped keep in hiding. Edward would not have been happy with these folk, as he continued to follow the presbyterian model of worship shaped by the Directory that had replaced the Church of England Prayer Book, with its space for extempore prayers and longer sermons. The local ministers would have met regularly to encourage and support one another, and some four times a year there would have been a gathering of the ministers and their congregations to participate in a grand-scale holy communion service, often spilling outdoors to accommodate the numbers.

But these ministers were beginning to have more worrying things on their minds. There was a new theological movement gathering strength in Parliament, not least since it was favoured by Oliver Cromwell. Known as Independency or Congregationalism, it not only rejected bishops but also the belief that the king was the head of the church.

James I's prophetic dictum "no bishops, no king" was becoming more likely to prove true by the day. The Independents wanted each church to govern itself, whilst the Presbyterians feared chaos and disorder if there were not a General Assembly and committees to order the church in the absence of bishops. Many Independents believed that the king, now captured and imprisoned by Parliament, would always impede this free and open church and oppose and undermine Parliament. There was talk of his being tried as a traitor to the country.

A strong principle of the puritan movement was that of fellowship between believers in general and the clergy in particular. The educated parish presbyter could easily be a somewhat lonely figure isolated from his fellows. The puritans stressed the need for clergy to have fellowship and meet together often. The group who met in the Banbury area, which included Edward, found themselves exercised by rumours about the future of the king. Their concerns culminated in a letter and a petition. On 21 January, 1648/9 a letter was sent to the presbyterian London ministers from 10 Oxfordshire ministers, including Edward Archer. In it they declared their intention to petition Lord Fairfax for the life of the king. Four days later, the eight-page petition was delivered to Lord Fairfax and published in London.[8]

"The Humble Advice and Earnest Desires of certain well-affected MINISTERS, lecturers of Banbury in the County of OXON, and of Brackly in the County of Northampton, to his Excellency, THOMAS Lord FAIRFAX, General of the Forces raised by the Authority of PARLIAMENT and to the General council of WARRE: Presented January 25, 1649, by two of the subscribers."

The ministers went on to thankfully acknowledge their debt to the Parliamentary Armies that had brought them *"in a fair way of being restored to a long desired enjoyment of our Religion and the Estates in freedom"*. Yet the trial and possible execution of the king was a different matter. The ministers declared that they were constrained to speak out because of *"our own Station Watchtower and give warning either of approaching sin or ruine to the Natione"*. They could not *"sit down in silence"* without *"wounding our own consciences, and betraying the trust reposed in us"*. They attacked the trial of the king on scriptural, historical, legal and moral grounds. It was, in essence, an appeal for the life of the king, whom the presbyterian ministers continued to believe was God's appointed representative on earth, and it was objecting to the ejection of presbyterian members of Parliament who would have opposed the arrest of the king. Fairfax was warned that when Edward II and Richard II had been deposed, a bloodbath had followed; and so the petition continued for more than 2,000 words.

As we know, the appeal went unheeded, the king was executed, and the Independent revolution now overtook the presbyterian one. Loyalty to the king was now declared traitorous. So, by signing this traitor's petition, Edward Archer suddenly found himself on the wrong side, and a focus for government spies. Almost certainly his preaching condemned the Parliament for the regicide, and was considered to be undermining the regime.

Edward's case did not come up in Parliament until 26 July, 1650 when, the State Papers[9] record, a letter was to be sent to the:

> "Militia Commissioners for the County of Oxford enclosing information against Mr. Archer, Minister of Somerton and desiring them to examine the charges against him and if they find the matter proved to prepare the charges against him and send him into safe custody."

That was followed up on 31 July with another letter from the Council of State to:

> "The committee for Plundered Ministers to send the examinations concerning Mr. Archer of Summerton (sic) county Oxford which will be returned when perused."

On 7 November, Edward petitioned the Council of State, and on 15 November the Council, having consulted the Committee for Plundered Ministers, ordered that Edward should take the Engagement (the oath of loyalty to the Republic), provide two sureties not under £100 each, appear before the council when summonsed, and be of good behaviour. All this must have been humiliating for a minister who had so recently been a rising star.

An entry for 5 December listed his two sureties as Thomas Justin of the city of Oxford, and Seth Ward of the university. The former was presumably a friendly puritan citizen able to stand surety for Edward; the second is of more significance, since Seth Ward had recently become Savilian Professor of Astronomy at Oxford, having gained a high reputation there by his theory of planetary motion. He was also currently engaged in a philosophical controversy with Thomas Hobbes. His willingness to stand surety for Edward suggests a common mind and some degree of friendship.

Some of Ward's scientific interests and studies may have attracted Edward, who had taken steps to make links with the university after his move to Somerton. Ward was no Presbyterian, however, and after the Restoration was a hardline bishop. But at this juncture the overwhelming revulsion to the death of the king must have swamped their lesser disagreements and bound them in opposition to the new regime. Also, Edward himself was surely re-evaluating his ideas about church in the light of his experiences.

Not surprisingly, since Parliament had many cases such as Edward's on its hands, and perhaps with Seth Ward's name on the papers, it decided to hand over the case to local jurisdiction. But not before it had seen that he was replaced at Somerton by a new Independent minister, John Fenwick.

Dec 18, "Order upon the petition of Edward Archer minister of Summerton [Somerton], County Oxon, that notwithstanding any former order of Council, his case be left to other proper judicature according to the rules given them by Parliament and it be declared to the petitioner that Council leaves him to make his defence before whom he shall be called to answer."

It appears that the case dragged on a further four years, after which the State Papers baldly record: "Edward Archer, Clerk of Somerton fined £200" (£20,000 today). That, of course, was a crippling amount that would hang over his head, although there was no real expectation that he would actually come up with such a sum. Neither is there any record of his having taken The Engagement.

Anthony Wood in his *Life and Times,* written almost a generation later, describes Edward as Edward of Newington, which was the parish he was appointed to after Somerton. Only the close-knit network of 17th century relationships can have enabled Wood to remember the insignificant parish where Edward ministered in the last years of the Protectorate. There is also an intriguing entry by Wood, writing on a flyleaf and apparently dated 1657: "Mr Archer minister of Newington concerning coynes". Woods, we know, was a keen numismatic, but Edward? Had he found coins, known of a collection, or was he himself a collector? Or was he trading in coins as a sideline? Either way, it was coins that put the two men in contact. Here, too, is another window into Edward having links with Oxford University, where he must have found congenial company.

To be appointed to Newington, Edward must have compromised or changed his views about Independency. Around Newington, the local family of note were the Doyleys. John Doyley, squire of Chiselhampton, was known as "a great friend of the gospel". He had been the MP for Oxford in the Long Parliament, but his royalist sympathies meant that he fell victim to Pride's Purge and was expelled in 1648. He would probably have remembered Edward from the time of the Long Parliament, and would have been sympathetic to his situation now that he was expelled from Somerton.

Newington was a quirky parish, being an Archdeacon's Peculiar whose patron was the Archbishop of Canterbury. The last incumbent had been Gilbert Sheldon, which Edward would come to rue. But for now, Sheldon, as a traditional churchman, was out of the scene and Newington was a hub of puritanism.

The complexities of the churches in this corner of Oxfordshire were legendary. In Newington was the parish church of St Giles, as well as a priory church left over from medieval times; Chiselhampton was technically a chapel of Stadhampton, and the patrons of St John the Baptist, Stadhampton, were the Doyley family. Each of the churches was within a mile of the others, and traditionally the curate of Stadhampton was also curate of Chiselhampton. The Doyleys had appointed Henry Owen as curate (later rector) to Stadhampton (then called Stodham!), and he shaped the parish into a puritan enclave. His son John grew up in Stadhampton and retained a house there, which he retired to after the Restoration when he married John Doyley's widow as his second wife. In 1657, the Doyleys appointed John Hartcliffe, Owen's brother-in-law, to the Stadhampton/Chiselhampton church. Clearly the Doyleys worked on the basis that anything to do with Owen was good.

So, how might Edward Archer have related to John Owen? One imagines that as a theologian and preacher he would have admired him. Owen challenged the theology of the Reformation for its lack of understanding of the Holy Spirit, who enabled Jesus to live a life of perfect harmony with the Father and whom believers must depend upon to live a holy life. Remembering that Edward looked for signs of the Spirit at work in Francis Pitt, it seems likely that Owen's theology of the Spirit would appeal to him. Owen was not merely a theologian, but also vice-chancellor of Oxford University as well as Cromwell's chief chaplain, so that he had the ear of the authorities in government and the university. Through his fellowship with the Owens and Doyleys of Stadhampton, Edward was drawn deep into the heart of the Cromwellian church.

It would have been understandable if Edward now looked forward to a quiet life. Newington was a tiny parish where he could concentrate on bringing up his growing family in peace and tranquillity, far from the turbulence of national politics, and hopefully recover his finances. By now, he had at least five children and four more would be born in Newington. Commonwealth registers for St Ethelburga, Leamington and Somerton no longer exist, but in that period we can deduce the birth of Edward, Ann, James, and Patience. The first three names are family ones, but Patience is a switch to a puritan name, and from then on the names of the children are all biblical.

The recorded births and baptisms for Edward and Mary's family are:

Mary, the first-born, baptised at Enville in 1641

Then from the Newington Registers:

1652 Benjamin, son of Edward, clerk and rector of Newington, 20 January
1654 Sarah, born and baptised on 26 October and buried 7 November
1656 Christian, baptised 6 May (born 6 April, being Easter Day) dt. Edward, rector
1657 Martha, 10 December (born 26 October) dt. Edward, rector

By this date, Edward was 45 and Mary was perhaps a year or two younger and menopausal – there were no more children.

No doubt the girls were given a basic education as well as learning to help in the glebe lands and house. Benjamin would be preparing for university from an early age, probably taught by his father and maybe members of John Owen's circle. Was it John Owen's influence as vice-chancellor of Oxford that opened the door for Benjamin to gain a place there? Significantly, his name was taken from the Bible account of Joseph's favoured younger son, and suggests that Edward and Mary saw their own youngest son in this light.

A further insight into Edward's accommodation with the new regime comes from finding his name in the records of the Triers, who were responsible for clergy appointments under Cromwell. In 1657, he certified John Richardson as a suitable minister of Fingest, Bucks. Alongside his signature were those of Ambrose Wethereld, vicar of Binfield, a highly political lawyer who described himself as a devoted son of the church, to which Anthony Wood commented "his religion was as venal as his tongue"; Edward Corbet, an older man who had been one of the Westminster Divines and very much in tune with Edward, whilst Oliver Cromwell was himself now the patron of Fingest. All these different strands and stances running through one appointment reveal the complexity of the Cromwellian church.[10]

Edward's tranquil life, with its godly fellowship in Newington, Stadhampton, and Chiselhampton, was not to last. On 3 September, 1658, Oliver Cromwell died. And just as the family were coming to terms with the implications of this event politically, their three-year-old Christian died on 14 February, 1659, the burial register recording her death.

On 13 March, 1659, a change of handwriting appears in the registers. At this stage, it was by no means certain whether presbyterianism might have a place in a restored national church, but it seems that Edward was being hounded out of Newington by more powerful clerics who had a vested interest in the parish. Two notes are inserted into the registers: "1650-9 Edward Archer, Pastor – intruded minister"; then in a later hand, "usurpation in ye rebellion against King Charles the first, Dr Sheldon being the lawful Rector".

On 23 June, 1660, a petition was delivered to the king asking that Edward Archer be replaced by Gilbert Sheldon, who had originally been made rector of Newington in 1639 by Archbishop Laud. Sheldon was a political and determined cleric who drew close to the king at court as soon as the royal party returned. Almost immediately, he was made Bishop of London. The king had great confidence in him. In October 1660, Sheldon was chosen to visit the regicides in prison, with the hope of gaining some sort of declaration of repentance from them. Unsurprisingly, then, when Archbishop Juxon died, Sheldon was appointed as his successor.

He had a portfolio of parishes already and certainly had no intention of returning to Newington as a parish priest, but since it was an archbishop's appointment he was able to suggest just the man to the king. In 1657, Sheldon's niece Catherine had married John Dolben , and Sheldon seized the moment to present Dolben to the parish.

So, on 15 November, 1660, John Dolben was instituted rector of Newington, first step to his climb to be the future Archbishop of York. However, the later chancery case detailed below includes eye-witnesses who testified that Edward was still active in the parish at Christmas and even into 1661, reflecting the anomalous situation many clergy found themselves in between 1660 and 1662. The Savoy Conference still hoped to produce an agreement that would enable the clergy who had continued to serve under Cromwell to be reconciled with a restored Church of England. Edward himself must have still been hoping for such a compromise, and to that end was open to another job in the national church.

Although he was not the sort of man to bow down to the hierarchy without a fight, at the end of the day, and certainly after 1662, he was in no position to stand up to Sheldon and Dolben, powerful figures who had the ear of the king. So, at some stage his wife must have once more supervised the transport of the household goods and the children, waved goodbye to their home of nearly a decade, and set off to seek refuge in a new parish away from the political spotlight that had now fallen on sleepy Newington.

Their destination was Cookham, on the banks of the Thames. It is likely that it was the presbyterian puritan network, and specifically Edward's friendship with its minister, that led to this move. The incumbent was William Hodson, whose family branch in England, in Houghton, Staffs, was said to have assisted Charles I's escape from Oxford in 1641. William, however, was from the Irish branch of the family, and since he served under the Commonwealth he must have come over from Ireland to get involved in the English revolution. We would know almost nothing about him, were it not for a letter that accompanied his resignation in April 1661 and was attached to his papers.[11]

"Whereas I received from Mr. George Weldon my noble patron the gift of the Vicaridge of Cookham, and being called away into Ireland by my Father doe give and deliver my Presentation, Donation and Collation after the space of Six months' time bearing date heretofore unto Mrs Mary Weldon if I return not againe and hold the said Vicaridge myself."

George Weldon was a puritan gentleman who had inherited the living. The Weldons had held the advowson since the Reformation, but George had no heir. So, he not only appointed William Hodson, but also bequeathed him the living when he died in 1659. There was an Irish branch of the Weldon family, suggesting that there may have been a link between the two families. But almost immediately, times changed again and neither Hodson, nor George's widow, Mary Weldon, could appoint a presbyterian. At this point, the Revd. John Hodson summonsed his son back home to Ireland, where the ecclesiastical scene was also changing fast. In 1660, John Hodson was appointed dean of Clogher and procured his son an appointment in the restored Irish Episcopal Church. William Hodson soon became rector of Annagh, where he settled and brought up his family. But when he first left England, he was still hedging his bets and did not immediately surrender the living.

In the meanwhile, Edward Archer had arrived in Cookham and taken over the church, presumably taking the tithes and fees whilst he did so. But what was his legal status in so doing? Indeed, what was the legal basis of the church between the return of the king and the final settlement in 1662? It was so full of grey areas that it became a minefield of irregularities in which neither Parliament nor the bishops were fully in charge. Once again, Edward Archer is seen to be tossed about by the uncertainty of the times – a phrase used time and time again in this period.

On 17 October, 1661, he appeared in a Chancery Case at Maidenhead, where he spoke on behalf of a parishioner and is described as a clerk of Cookham.[12] Then on 31 October, he solemnised a wedding at Cookham between Sara Atkins, a widow of Cookham, and Richard Clarke of Great Marlow. No banns were read nor was a licence sought. Was Edward being truculent, saving the couple money, or had the breakdown in the church's administration meant that Edward had simply ceased to bother with canon law?

Soon after the 1662 settlement, a Visitation of Buckingham was conducted and many such irregularities came to light. The Clarkes were to be fined for their indiscretion, but pleaded poverty as an excuse for not paying. However, the vicar of Great Marlow, John Furnes, was recently appointed and zealous for the restored church. He pointed out that Richard Clarke kept "an Inn at the sign of the barne" in Marlow, and could not therefore be considered poor. The Visitation would also expose the irregularities in Edward's position.

Meanwhile, on 11 November, 1661, William Hodson stuck to his agreement and resigned from Cookham; the restored regime was catching up with the intruded ministers and replacing them with clergy who were not tainted by "the rebellion". So, Francis Crawley was appointed by Bishop Humphrey Henchman on the very same day that Hodson resigned, as though he was poised to pounce. Crawley had been ordained in 1645 at Trinity College chapel, and had been waiting for a restoration since then.

This brought Edward and family one step nearer the final crisis; the imminent passing of the Act of Uniformity, whereby the Solemn

League and Covenant was to be adjured by all the incumbents of England under penalty of losing their livings. For Edward and many of his contemporaries, the Covenant had reflected all they believed in about the reform of the church and all they had suffered for in supporting it. There would be no compromise for the 3,000 ejected ministers who now left the Church of England.

The celebrated historian of the Great Ejection, Calamy, writes the following about Edward Archer:

"When he was cast out of his benefice in 1662 he had little or no provision for their sustenance; yet he died in the belief that providence would take care of those he left behind, telling his wife that she 'needed not to be anxious for her children for God would not suffer her or them to want'. Which proved true. He left a son who was a conforming minister at Quainton in Bucks."[13]

God's provision, however, was not without considerable assistance from Edward's resourceful nature. On the principle that God helps those who help themselves, in 1663/4 Edward took legal proceedings to recover tithes he believed he was owed from his days in Newington. The first hearing before Sir Robert Lyde at Oxford Assizes was lost, and Lyde pronounced in favour of Sheldon, who then sued Edward for possession of the rectory and won once again.[14]

Hard-pressed financially, Edward now made another attempt to recover Newington tithes from a wealthy widow, Mary Dunche.[15] The Dunches were a settled and prominent local family, some of whom had been MPs. They were parliamentarians and indeed some were related to Cromwell. So, there is no suggestion that Edward was taking advantage of a poor widow, but rather that he had a legitimate grievance with a powerful local family. Once again, he seems to pick his fights with the powerful. Does this suggest a radical streak in him that took the side of the poor against the oppressor, or was this simply the consequence of living in the inequalities of 17th century society?

The case was to be heard before the High Court of the Exchequer chamber at Westminster. No record of the verdict seems to be extant, and it may well be that there was an out-of-court settlement. What the case has left us with is a number of confirmatory details about Edward's life. Depositions were taken at the sign of the Bull, Dorchester, Oxon and posted in chambers at Oxford and Westminster.

How old was he? Some said 50 in 1651, others between 40 and 50.

When and where was he ordained? Daniel, a labourer, sayth that he has heard that the complainant was ordained a minister by the Bishop of Lichfield and Coventry about 35 yrs. since and that he doth believe him to be between 40 and 50.

When was he instituted to Newington parsonage and church and how long did he live there? Some say 1651, others confirm he was resident from 1655–60 and that he was there on 25 December, 1660, whilst others testify that he was still there in 1661.

What tithes did he receive? Much detail about poultry, wools, turkeys, and pyggies followed.

Did he perform the duties of a minister? Yes, but there were some questions about the frequency of the Sacrament of the Lord's Supper and thus his entitlement to oblations and offerings linked to it.

Now without a job or income, Edward had to be newly resourceful. He stayed in Cookham, rented premises, and opened a brewery. In 1662, he was assessed for Hearth Tax on his property, suggesting busy and productive premises with much coming and going of employees, as well as the children who were surely involved in this family affair. Edward must have relied heavily on his wife (50), and children Mary (21), Martha (c.20), Patience (c.20) and son Benjamin (10). James and Edward had probably left home, and daughter Anne had died in 1663 and was buried in Cookham churchyard. She is described as the daughter of "Mr. Edward Archer, clerk" in the Cookham register.

These were to be his hidden years, when he concentrated on making a living and bringing up the family. After a lifetime of litigation, petitioning, and preaching, he appears to have withdrawn totally from the world of politics and religion. However, one wonders whether he was too quiet! Would he really have surrendered the militant attitude of a lifetime so easily? We know that many of the ejected ministers conducted secret services in their premises, and Edward's house would have been ideal for a small gathering of puritan believers. The 12 chairs in the kitchen were more than the family's need, so Christian hospitality was suggested by that symbolic number. This would not have been a large gathering that would have brought upon it the attention of the authorities, but by meeting as an extended family gathering, Edward could have both fulfilled his ministry and stayed just within the boundaries of the law. He would argue that this was more like friends and family gathering for prayers than any sort of church.

Compton's Census of 1676 recorded 641 Church of England members in Cookham. This cannot have meant just the village, but probably included all the Maidenhead chapelry. There were 16 Roman Catholics and 30 non-conformists. The editor has appended a note to explain this high figure from *Lyon Turner, Original records of Early Non-Conformity,* stating that in 1669 there was a conventicle in Cookham. However, this turns out to be led by Anabaptists who were licensed to hold services locally. This would be far too extreme for Edward, surely, or might he have toyed with such ideas in his distress? So maybe the family simply retreated into themselves, worshipped informally at home, and dutifully attended the parish church for appearances' sake.

After Edward's death, the family continued to worship as non-conformists. The only one we know of who definitely did not tread the non-conformist path was Benjamin, who must have realised that if he was to be of any influence in society and the church he must conform. Did his father approve? He must have supported him to go to Oxford, which began his conformist pathway when he signed up at Exeter College Oxford in 1670, and both Edward and Benjamin were described as plebs of Cookham, Berks.[16] One imagines that this was as big a struggle as any in Edward's turbulent life. Could he deny his son the same opportunity that he had had in going to university? But could he equally accept the fact that this meant Benjamin must now conform? Yet, had not Edward himself been ordained in the established church, even though that had been a time when radical change was still on the cards? Could those hopes of change ever return? Might toleration win the day? Therefore, should not Benjamin conform and wait patiently for the restoration of puritan hopes within the established church?

Edward would not live to see how the church did change in many ways, but not entirely as the puritans had hoped. In 1672, he left this world of conflicts, and was buried in Cookham churchyard on 20 February as "Mr. Edward Archer, clerk".

Edward's widow lived on for another 14 years, blessed by an expanding family. In 1672, Patience Archer wed Thomas Simms, a yeoman of Stadhampton. It was 10 years since the family had left Newington, yet it was there that Patience found her husband and where they settled. The status of yeoman was not high, though it held a sense of respectability and ancient roots in the land, and could be considered a suitable match for the daughter of an ejected minister. The next year, Mary Simms – the first grandchild – was baptised in Chiselhampton.

In 1674, on 20 January, "Mr Edward Archer from London" was buried at Cookham. Presumably, this was Edward and Mary's son who returned to his mother when dying. We know nothing else about him.

In 1675, the Revd. James Archer of Yardley – Edward's father – was buried.

Not until 28 August, 1676, was Edward's estate finally settled by an Administration,[17] since he had not left a will. It was valued at £650 (£86,000 in today's prices). The Administration revealed a comfortable lifestyle in a roomy house. All the bedrooms had feather beds and bolsters and chests; the kitchen was well equipped; the study had turkey carpets, a desk with cash and bonds, and a library worth £80. Then there were all the accoutrements for brewing beer, including quantities of barley and mash ready for fermentation. Outside were tools for husbandry, along with a sty with pigs and piglets.

His children were given appropriate portions. Patience received £50 retrospectively as her wedding portion. Benjamin, now a fellow of Exeter College, received £30 towards his maintenance. Mary, Sarah, and Martha were each given £24, which was calculated to support them for four-and-a-half years. After debts and funeral expenses, Mary was left with some £60,000 in today's money, for her future life. Apparently, the family had continued to rent their home in Cookham until the estate was settled, but now Mary moved a few miles north to Beaconsfield where she would live with her unmarried daughters for her final 10 years on earth.

The settlement and move may have precipitated daughter Mary's marriage to William Segory. She was 42 and he was 61 years. Calamy struggles to be positive about him, but says he had a gentle side. Otherwise, he appears as a somewhat dry and crusty old puritan bachelor, who ran a school in Wokingham after being ejected in 1662. He had a reputation for being a fierce disciplinarian when he was at Oxford. He and Mary supported the Dissenting Meeting House in Wokingham.

Mary Archer died in 1686 and her PCC will is, as ever, a window into the person we have known little of until her death. It gives us a cameo of the family as it now stood. Royalist like her husband, she loyally acknowledges King James II, perhaps blissfully unaware of the troubles he would shortly bring upon the nation. She commits her soul to the undivided Trinity, perhaps a deliberate rejection of spreading Socinian views and a firm declaration of her own orthodox faith, which is also expressed in her declaration that she trusts only in Christ's merits for everlasting bliss. Her unusual stress on the Trinity may also reflect her own engagement with the works of John Owen, whom she, too, would have met and heard preach at Stadhampton.

There are modest legacies to her children: Patience Simms, £10; and £10 to granddaughter Susanna. Martha, who is about to marry, would receive household goods worth some £40 or so. James and his wife Sarah, otherwise unheard of, are remembered and left ten shillings each. Traditional mourning rings are to be provided for all her children. Benjamin is to be her executor. She calls him her "dear and beloved son" with a sense of pride that suggests his conformity was no longer or never had been an issue for her. The poor of Beaconsfield are left 40 shillings.

In the parish burial register for Beaconsfield, Mary Archer carries the title Mrs, in contrast to the normal use of Christian name and surname only. In spite of her husband's ejection, it seems she had retained her dignity and status, perhaps by dint of her sheer determination and personality.

Edward Archer began life as an enthusiastic minister of the puritan persuasion. He embraced presbyterian views and remained a committed royalist. With the country plunged into civil war, he hurried to London to be at the centre of the new presbyterian experiment backed by Parliament. But he gradually became disillusioned with the way the war was going, and asked Parliament to release him from St Ethelburga's and appoint him to a quieter country parish. He went to Leamington and later to Somerton. Here the impending execution of the king caused him to join those who were petitioning Parliament not to execute their sovereign. Thus, he incurred the displeasure of Parliament, leading to a hefty fine and the loss of his parish.

From now on, he was dependent on friends and contacts to survive with his family and to have a job. His going to Newington appears to have been brought about by the goodwill of the Doyley family, and maybe their mentor John Owen, and Seth Ward. Then came the Restoration, when clergy ejected in the 1640s moved in to reclaim their parishes. At this point, Edward moved to Cookham where an old friend was the vicar, where he provided cover until his friend chose to stay in Ireland and resign the living.

The 1662 Act of Uniformity was the end of the road for Edward's ministerial career and he now had to earn his living as a maltser and smallholder. Alas, we have no firm evidence about the level of his faith and wellbeing by the end of his life, except that his son Benjamin, who grew up under his influence, went on to pursue a clerical calling. And Calamy includes Edward in his biographies of rejected ministers, with an upbeat paragraph about his faith in God's provision for his family when he died.

In his lifetime, we know Edward was involved in a number of conflicts. There were the issues surrounding the lunatic vicar at Enville. There was his pamphlet about what happened at Rushall. Signing the petition for the wellbeing of the King was another provocative act. There were his tithe cases after his expulsion from Newington. Was he by nature litigious, or were most of these cases the result of the Civil War, which he was caught up in against his will?

Sources

1. Parish Registers still exist for Yardley, Enville, Newington, Stadhampton, Cookham, and Beaconsfield.
2. Venn's *Alumni Cantabria* and Foster's *Alumni Oxon*

Notes

1. *Staffordshire Incumbents and Parochial Records, 1530–1680*, Ed. W N Landor, William Salt Library, Staffordshire. (WSAS 99)
   The Bishop's subscription book does not record the Enville appointment until 1637; *Subscription Book* LRO B/A/4/18 [CCEd]
2. Visitation of Lichfield, 1635 L.J.R.O.B/V/1 p7
3. Petition to Laud PRO, State Papers 16 255.

4. *The English Clergy 1558–1642,* R O' Day
5. The St Ethelburga appointment is recorded in the *Journal of the House of Commons*, House of Lords Record Office, 20 March, 1643.
6. *A More Exact and Perfect Relation of the Treachery, Apprehension, Conviction etc. of Francis Pitt 1644*, William Salt Library. It was reprinted in 1881. It also exists as a Thomason tract in the British Library as well as a variety of American universities.
7. Commonwealth Registers. The Leamington appointment appears in the records of the Committee for Plundered Ministers (British Library).
8. Humble Petition of Banbury. I have found only a transcript made in the 1960s by Ronald Archer Claydon in an unpublished history. He clearly saw it but I cannot trace it.
9. The charges against him at Somerton in 1650 are all in the Calendar of State Papers for the period and as these are indexed, the story can be easily traced. *Blomfield's History of the Bicester Deanery* also summarises them (Vol. 4, p41).
10. Fingest. I am grateful to Rebecca Warren of Kent University, who is currently researching the Cromwellian church, for this information.
11. Hodson's letter is reproduced in his CCEd entry for Cookham citing W & SRO D1/14/1/1a Ordination Papers.
12. See *Chancery Depositions before 1714,* in the Genealogical Soc-SP/CHA 432 222/60.
13. Calamy, *Nonconformist Memorials* 1775, ii p310 and *Calamy Revised*, Mathews 1934, OUP.
14. Another discovery by R A Claydon without surviving citation.
15. Tithe dispute. The tithes case is at Kew PRO; E 134 Chas2 15 and 16. Hil. 3 as an original document.
16. Foster, *Alumni Oxon.*
17. Administration and inventory of Edward Archer, *Berkshire Wills and Administrations.*

Benjamin Archer (1652–1733):
Third Generation

Benjamin Archer grew up as the youngest son of a minister in the Cromwellian church. He was the only Archer who was not nurtured on the Book of Common Prayer. He was born in 1652 and baptised on 20 January at St Giles, Newington[1] where his father was the rector. The choice of his name seems significant, since the biblical Benjamin was a much doted-upon youngest son. There were to be eight comparatively comfortable years at Newington where young Benjamin would have been exposed to an Independent-style worship in his father's church.

His education would have begun from his early years, with him probably being taught by his father. He learned Latin and Greek, maths, English and, of course, the Bible. At times, no doubt, some of his father's many friends tutored him for a while. He was a quick learner and everyone agreed that it would be good for him to go to university, after which he would end up as a minister, a lawyer, or an academic – but he could make up his mind later.

His sisters, Martha, Mary, and Patience, dutifully helped their mother around the house, and although they would have learned to read and write, their future expectations were confined to marriage or remaining at home helping their parents. Benjamin's older brothers visited occasionally but had little impact on his life.

When he was six, there was much talk of a man called Oliver Cromwell who had died, and now everyone was worried about what would happen next. Some thought the solution lay in the return of the king: not the one who had been executed, but his son Charles. Although Benjamin's father believed in the monarchy, he did not like what happened next. Even before the king came back, people began to visit Newington, and apparently they were important men and the eight-year-old Benjamin watched them go into his father's study. Afterwards, his father seemed very preoccupied, and before long he gathered the family together and told them that they would have to leave Newington very soon. But they were not to worry, because there was a friend of the family who was vicar of a lovely Thameside town called Cookham and he had to go to Ireland, so Edward would be looking after his church for a while and they could all go and live in the vicarage.

So came the family's departure to Cookham, where for a short while Edward continued to minister as a sort of informal locum. Benjamin liked being so near the river and found moving quite exciting, but he noticed that his father became very moody. News from London would sometimes lift him up, and at other times send him into gloomy silence. Benjamin worked out that there were discussions and conferences going on about the future of the church. There was some hope that the non-conformist clergy would be allowed to continue in their ministry alongside the returning Church of England ministers. But the day came when Benjamin was told that the bishops had won and all clergy would have to swear allegiance to their authority, which was something that Edward could not in all conscience now do. So, the family would be homeless and poor, and Edward would have to find a job, and Benjamin was now man enough to help support the family.

So, after 1662, Edward joined the ejected clergy and henceforth the family had to earn their keep practically. Edward rented a rambling property and, thanks to the detailed administration at the time of his death, we have a vivid picture of the family's life in Cookham.[2] The chief room in the house was the parlour, with two tables and a dozen leather chairs, six with cushions. There was a court cupboard, three carpets on the floor, and a spacious fireplace with a shovel and tongs. On the mantelpiece was a brass clock and some choice pieces of silver plate. There was a board containing bills and debts valued at £270

(£28,000 in today's money). There was also a dining hall with a table and 12 iron stools with a massive brass furnace, in front of which stood a pair of andirons and dogs.

Mary Archer and her daughters, probably with servants, too, worked in the kitchen and buttery with a half hogshead flour barrel and a tub to mix the bread. There were vessels and measures for brewing beer, three iron pots, potholders, pot hangers, 24 pewter dishes, a dozen pewter plates, two pewter basins, one pewter flagon, a warming pan, shovel and tongs, a smoothing iron, a skimmer, and a brass mortar. Also on the ground floor Edward had his large library, valued at £80 (£80,000) in today's money, which would eventually find its way to his descendants.

Upstairs were ample bedrooms (chambers), the main one being above the parlour where Edward and Mary slept. It had a double bedstead with lace and serge curtains and valances, a feather mattress, feather bolster, three blankets, two carpets, two tables, two chairs, and a fireplace with andirons, dogs, and a shovel. In the girls' room was an oak chest containing 24 sheets, 12 flax tablecloths, 36 flaxen napkins, 24 hemp napkins, diaper tablecloths and napkins, curtains, valances, carpets and mantels, and other wearing apparel – it must have been a very big chest! Each of the three beds had feather mattresses and bolsters, together with pillows, blankets, and coverlets.

Benjamin would be the sole occupant of the boys' bedroom, with bed, cupboard, three chairs and several stools, described as "finely wrought".

In the stables outside the house Edward kept a bay nag and a cart, a cow, a hog, and a sow that had recently given birth to piglets. There were tools of husbandry, piles of logs, and a number of hayricks. Also on Edward's land was a malt house and a mill powered by a stream flowing into the Thames. Edward seems to have been a surprisingly successful maltser and smallholder, given the comfortable state of his home when he died.

As a teenager and the only son at home, Benjamin must have been busy helping in the brewing and husbandry through which his family now survived. Family prayers would have continued, and Benjamin may have noticed that more and more people joined them. Perhaps his father was soon in his stride as a preacher once again, even though it was illegal for him to run a church. They would all have had to be careful not to sing too loudly and to leave by different entrances at different times. As a teenager, Benjamin was party to this unconventional lifestyle, though he knew his mother was worried that his father might be arrested. On Sundays and feast days, the family all attended the parish church although they grumbled about it afterwards. But if they did not do this, then they were likely to be fined, and if Benjamin was to go to university this conformity was necessary.

What with the beer and the pigs, it is not surprising that Benjamin's education fell behind. It would be normal to go to university between the ages of 14 and 16, but Benjamin was 18 before he made it to Oxford, finally throwing in his lot with the Restoration Settlement, since joining the university required the taking of formal oaths to the crown and the church. Oxford was the nearer of the two English universities and the one where his father now had the most contacts, although he himself was a Cambridge man.

This made Benjamin the only Archer clergyman not to attend Cambridge. He matriculated in May 1670 at Pembroke College, and was registered as a *Pleb. Son of Edward*, also a Pleb.[3] They were at the bottom of the social ladder. Benjamin's position was further weakened by the death of his father two years later. When Edward's Administration came through in 1676, it included maintenance money for Benjamin at college as well as marriage portions for his sisters. He obtained his BA in 1673/4 and is recorded as a Batellar 20 April-6 July,[3] suggesting that he was still very poor, though almost immediately he was appointed a fellow of Exeter College, so he must have been spotted and now could earn his keep through an income from pupils.

Two important men now shaped his life. One was the Master of

Exeter, Arthur Bury, and the other the newly consecrated Bishop of Oxford, John Fell. The bishop was searching out men for ordination, and Benjamin was duly ordained deacon on 11 March, 1677.[4] Apparently, he was also awarded his MA on the same date as the ordination, which was in Christchurch Cathedral, so perhaps the ceremonies were coupled up.

Fell was an orthodox and charismatic man who took a personal interest in his ordinands and would have followed Benjamin's progress, or lack of it. He was also a disciplinarian who put fear into the hearts of careless students. One wrote a ditty to express his fear of the disciplinarian doctor:

> I do not love thee Dr Fell
> The reason why I cannot tell;
> But this I know and know full well,
> I do not love thee, Dr Fell.

Why these four lines should have attained legendary status I cannot tell, but they have, and I became aware of them in my own childhood, assuming Dr Fell was a scary medical man! Fell was a typical post-Restoration clergyman, deeply hostile to Roman Catholicism. He was also a King's Chaplain with access to the royal ear.

Benjamin was not priested for four years, until 27 March, 1682,[4] when Bishop John Fell and others laid hands upon him in Christchurch Cathedral. Since Benjamin was not planning to take a parish and surrender his fellowship, there was no urgency about his priesting. Nevertheless, the gap gives food for thought about what was going on in his mind at this time. More enigmatic still is a comment of the diarist Anthony Wood for 26 August, 1683: "A bawdy sermon at St Mary's in the afternoon by Benjamin Archer of Exeter, son of Archer of Newington."[5] Wood was not at the sermon himself so gives us no more information. But what are we to make of the word bawdy? Wood appears to have been on good terms with Archer so it is unlikely that it was a criticism outright. Could it be jokey, comparing Benjamin with the court wits whose language was often on the edge of the socially acceptable? Or was it a more pointed reference to contemporary politics and expressing support for the Whigs, with their acceptance of the non-conformists, in a rumbustious and earthy manner?

Perhaps Benjamin was more gung-ho at this time because he was about to take on a parish. Not that he was yet ready to give up his fellowship, so he must have worked out a way of maintaining his involvement at Exeter College whilst serving his new parish of Wexham in Bucks, not many miles from Windsor.

On 28 November, 1683, he was licensed as a preacher and instituted as rector of Wexham.[6] The patron was the crown, King Charles II, but it is pretty certain that the post was given at the request of Richard Winwood, MP for Windsor and a longstanding friend of Benjamin's father. Winwood had been an MP in the Long Parliament and attended many of the ecclesiastical committees that Parliament set up. He remained an enthusiastic presbyterian all his life. He would have been familiar with Edward, both in his London ministry and in the subsequent parishes to which Parliament had appointed him.

Richard Winwood was now 74, but not too old to offer support to his old friends. The Winwoods lived in Ditton Park between Windsor and Wexham , but were also Lords of the Manor of Quainton, Bucks, where Richard Winwood was the patron of the church. Winwood was typical of the post-Restoration gentry who had lived through the Civil War and emerged unhappy with the ecclesiastical settlement, but rather than fan the flames of further hostilities had lived quietly on their estates where they could worship as they preferred. Just as Roman Catholic gentry had their priests, the presbyterians and Independents had their chaplains. Outwardly, they conformed to the settlement of 1662, attending their parish church with their families and taking the sacrament four times a year.

Many gentry were also owners of one or more advowsons, and were able to appoint clergy close to their own convictions. For the Presbyterians, their ideal would be a young man formed in the days of the Commonwealth, from a presbyterian family. The network of relationships forged in presbyterian times remained active behind the scenes after the Restoration. There is no evidence to show exactly when Benjamin became Winwood's chaplain, but it probably coincided with his appointment to Wexham. The first reference to Benjamin living with the Winwoods comes in July 1687 when Anthony Wood, the Oxford diarist and antiquarian, sent a letter to Benjamin at Ditton Park, the Winwoods' estate, asking for information about Sir Ralph Winwood and Edward Bulstrode of Upton, Slough; it was no secret where to find Benjamin. Meanwhile, Winwood was repairing and endowing the Chapel of the Assumption on his estate, and in his will he gives Benjamin the choice of whether to live in the great brick house (where Winwood had kept his hawks) for £30 p.a. or find his own accommodation for £50 p.a.

Hitherto, Benjamin had lived in the Winwood manor with the family where, as stipulated in Winwood's will, he had his own rooms, was provided with food, had his washing done for him, and all the candles he needed were supplied. This arrangement was to continue, although Winwood may have known that Benjamin's bachelor state was not to last much longer.

About the same time that Benjamin moved to Wexham, his eldest sister Mary got married at the age of 42. Her husband, the Revd. William Segory, was an academic, much older than herself, and currently living in Wokingham where he pastored a successful non-conformist meeting house since, like Mary's father, he was one of the ejected ministers of 1662. He was not considered to be a lively preacher. However, the couple would be a respectable and staid influence on the people of Wokingham, as they gave themselves to a dissenting ministry in one of the country's registered chapels. Ironically, greater toleration was on the horizon following the death of Charles II in 1685, when his brother James, openly a Roman Catholic, ascended to the throne. James favoured religious toleration since it would legitimise his promoting and favouring of Roman Catholics.

In response, many erstwhile presbyterians and Independents of the Commonwealth days were beginning to emerge into what would later become a distinct political party, the Whigs. Families like the Winwoods would join the Whigs to protect the interests of Protestantism and the non-conformists. Richard Winwood wrote to his brother-in-law, who eventually became his heir, delighted that the Montague family had selected a presbyterian-minded chaplain who was the son of another of the ejected ministers of 1662, just as Richard had chosen Benjamin Archer. The extended family were part of the hidden presbyterian network that was a counterpart to the Roman Catholic recusants.

In 1686, Benjamin's mother Mary died in her home in Beaconsfield, leaving a no-nonsense will of which her "dear and beloved son" Benjamin was the sole executor. There was a little money for all her living children, and household goods to her married daughters. She was accorded the title Mrs Archer in the burial register, indicating that social respect remained constant even for those who had been on the wrong side at the Restoration.

In 1688, Benjamin gained his third degree, a BD, making him well able to engage in concentrated theological debate, which he would shortly be called upon to do. Perhaps it was in recognition of his attainment that he was appointed catechista for Exeter College in June that year. Not that many people would have noticed the appointment – instead, all eyes were fixed on Holland, since many English leaders had issued an invitation to the House of Orange to take over the monarchy. James II fled, William and Mary arrived, and the comparatively bloodless "Glorious Revolution" changed the direction of the country. There were also immediate consequences for Benjamin and his colleagues at Exeter College.

One of the prime movers in the revolution was Sir Jonathan Trelawny, who was a clergyman as well as a knight. Apparently, he had long had his eye upon the bishopric of Exeter and soon had the pleasure of realising his aspirations. Only three days after the coronation of William and Mary, 13 April, 1689, Exeter was allotted to him, and his nomination by the new king was swiftly confirmed. In June 1689, he set out to Exeter, but in his progress to the great see of the West, he made a formal visitation to Exeter College, which fell under his jurisdiction as bishop.

The Victorian historian Agnes Strickland vividly reconstructed this visitation[7] in striking and sonorous prose. Very stormy was the reception he met with there, she says. Exeter College was not only malcontent but mutinous, and the bishop's approach raised something like an insurrection, as the fellows were divided for and against him. The rector of the college, Dr Arthur Bury, with a strong party of the fellows, hostilely encountered the bishop in the open quadrangle, and there protested vehemently against his nearer approach.

Feelings ran high when the new bishop and his supportive fellows, and the rector with all his refractory fellows, got together into the hall. Everybody's orthodoxy or moral character was impugned, and everybody had the advantage of having his sins confessed in sonorous Latin very audibly by his neighbour. Indeed, much good Latin was likewise expended in tracts and handbills, which had been prepared for the arrival of the new bishop, and vigorously all the fellows of Exeter scolded each other in that learned language.

A number of factors fuelled the debates. Some were still unable to accept the new king and still viewed James, for all their dislike of him, as the Lord's anointed. Bound up with this divide was the growing political divide in the country between Whigs and Jacobite's; one or the other affiliation being in every individual's heart. Finally, questions of orthodoxy in religion were ideal weapons to fling at the other party. Theology by definition explores new insights, but the mind of the orthodox Exeter College was wavering upon the heresy of Socinianism. Such was the colourful and picturesque language employed by Strickland, declaiming that "party rage loured on every brow, while sins against orthodoxy, and lower scandals even, were shouted by every tongue".

Apparently, Bishop Sir Jonathan Trelawney conducted himself in the midst of the uproar in the most gentlemanly manner. The only interruption he gave to Dr Arthur Bury – who had some very vituperant Latin protest to read against his authority – was to request him to sit down instead of standing while he read it in the hall. But even that request was interpreted as a provocation, and Arthur Bury is said to have refused the courtesy with the neat repartee, "No, I will stand by what I say." Yet, soon after, he placed his protestation in the hands of one of the fellows of his party to read, and flung himself contemptuously out of the hall. In the hubbub that followed, very little could be heard of what the reading "fellow" had to utter.

Benjamin Archer stood firmly alongside his rector; whether for emotional or intellectual reasons is not clear, but probably a blend of both. Trelawny's Visitation was made on 16 April. At the college annual meeting on 30 June, Benjamin was re-appointed catechista and bursar. But in July, the bishop finally took action to establish his authority, and on 24 July the rector was expelled and Benjamin was among those fellows who in August were suspended for their behaviour, *"Propter contemptuart"*.[8]

In the spring of 1690, Arthur Bury published *The Naked Gospel*, an appeal for freeing the gospel from academic disputations and to concentrate on its essence of repentance and faith. He asked some challenging questions about the Trinity and described academic disputations about God as "boys' play". He did not entirely reject the traditions of the church but suggested that over-inquisitiveness about the exact nature of God, along with the growing prosperity of the early church, had made Christians wanton and led them into fierce disputacity.

From the explosion of pamphlets throughout the Civil War, there had been plentiful challenges about returning to the primitive church, and this quest remained foremost in theological discussion. If Bury had not been in trouble already, his writing might have passed unnoticed as one more contemporary exploration of the gospel. However, it was seized upon by the authorities as heretical and labelled Socinian at a time when Oxford was riven with disputes about the Trinity. It took the authorities five years to get rid of Bury, but they succeeded in the end.

The fact that Benjamin took Bury's side suggests that he was himself open-minded and questioning rather than a hard-line traditionalist. Whether he agreed with everything Bury wrote, we can't be sure, but he must have believed that this was a legitimate theological exploration. But by now he had been part of Oxford University for 20 years, during which time it had been his home and in many ways his family. He was ready for a change. As a Fellow, he could have stayed there all his life as long as he was prepared not to marry. His suspension left him in a dilemma, and must have led him to consider his other option of marriage and a more substantial parish ministry. Wexham may have been a useful counterbalance to the intensity of college life, but it was not ideal for a full-time calling with an income of only five pounds and 15 shillings a year.

In 1687, Richard Winwood died and his estate passed to his sister and her husband, as the Winwoods had no children. His will deals swiftly with his estate and goes into great detail about the almshouses to be built at his other manor of Quainton, for which he leaves a considerable sum both to build and fund them. The rector of Quainton was to have a big say in their running. An equal amount of space is devoted to the future of the chapel in the grounds of the manor house in which he had lived in Ditton Park. Originally it had been a medieval chantry that he had recently finished repairing and refurbishing. He recommends continuing the arrangement that he and Benjamin had already agreed upon, but gave his wife freedom over the housing of her chaplain, noting that the repairs to the chapel included a house for the chaplain. He wants the chapel to purchase a flagon, chalice, and paten, but recommends that these are kept safe in the house. The chapel is to be provided with books, seats, and cushions, and kept in good repair. If more ornaments are to be bought, then his trustees must all agree on them. The money for this would come from his investment in the New River taking water into the heart of London. Many other named parishes were to receive money for their poor from this lucrative investment.

There is no record of Winwood's chapel ever being licensed. Meanwhile, Benjamin was clearly bound up in this scheme as Winwood's chaplain. He seemed to have a foot in both camps. As rector of Wexham, he conformed to the established church, and as Winwood's chaplain he could take less rigidly prescribed services. Alas, no records of Benjamin's sermons from this time exist; perhaps these were amongst the papers that he asked to be burned after his death. As it happened, not only did Winwood's death change his situation, but the coming of William and Mary the following year paved the way to a new relationship between the state and non-conformist sympathisers, like Benjamin, within the established church.

Before he died, Richard Winwood had promised Benjamin the parish of Quainton, of which he was patron, when it next became vacant. Knowing the vacancy might not occur in his own lifetime, he ensured that this would happen by granting the next appointment to his close friend and colleague George Evelyn, cousin of the diarist, John Evelyn. George Evelyn, too, had sat in the Long Parliament until excluded by Pride's Purge. After the Restoration, he resumed his parliamentary career as MP for Surrey. Evelyn would also have remembered Edward Archer from Commonwealth days. He would know that Richard Winwood had favoured Benjamin's appointment, and so George duly presented him to Quainton when the vacancy there occurred. Benjamin was instituted and inducted as rector in March 1690.

With an annual income of £30.12.1d and a large comfortable rectory, Quainton provided a secure base for family life. Six months later, he was joined at the rectory by his new bride, Ann Ingelo, née Evans. It is probable that Richard Winwood also had a hand in this arrangement. As MP for New Windsor, he would know the clergy in St George's Chapel in the castle. One, Canon George Evans, stood out as a presbyterian sympathiser with a feisty daughter whose first husband had died, leaving her a young widow with a small son. Benjamin and Ann wed in the tiny parish of Hitcham, where Canon Evans was the Rector in tandem with his work at Windsor Castle. George Evans officiated at the service, which took place on 8 September, 1692. The groom was 40, the bride 34. Benjamin had gained an experienced clergy wife, her jointure from her first marriage, the support of a significant churchman, and 10 brothers- and sisters-in-law, all of whom were people of conviction and mostly clergy or clergy wives.

Ann's siblings included Mary, married to William Stonestreet, rector of St Stephen's, Walbrook; Thomas Evans, fellow of Eton; Jane now a Mountague, whose husband had an Eton living in the West Country; and her eldest brother George, rector of St Benet Fink. Ann's father-in-law from her first marriage, Dr Ingelo, had been provost of Eton under the Commonwealth, and remained a fellow there. He had married into a Quaker family and Ann may have imbibed some Quaker teaching from her life within the Ingelo circle before she met Benjamin.

The Ingelos were musical, which saved them from the purges of the Restoration, since Ingelo and Purcell produced an anthem for the king's return. Ann, too, shared their love of music. Benjamin must have been happy to have a wife with some spark and challenge that echoed his own aspirations for a more open and radical protestant church. But he was a cautious man, and did not lightly let go of his Oxford life. Ironically, his fellowship at Exeter College was restored, and we read of him being elected subrector and prolector of theology in 1691 and again in 1692. It was not until 1 December, 1692, that he formally and finally resigned from the college. Perhaps he found it hard to let go, and the college leaned on him after its disturbing upheavals and schisms. But maybe it was the birth of his first child, Ann, who was baptised at Quainton on 2 February, 1692/3, that sealed his final move from Oxford and the beginning of serious parochial ministry.

Benjamin's life falls into two halves. The first half reflected the turbulent days of the Civil War, the uncertainties around the Restoration, and the continuing tensions in the nation until finally the Glorious Revolution brought about a level of religious toleration that was at least acceptable, if not ideal. In the first quarter of his life, Benjamin lived under the shadow of being the son of an ejected minister. The next quarter was spent in Oxford where he succeeded academically, became a Fellow, and got ordained without any apparent intention of settling down as a parish priest. He clearly mastered the art of meeting the right people, and we get the impression of a charming and interesting man rising above the situation his family had fallen into.

The second half of his life was built around his own growing family and a faithful ministry at Quainton. He and Ann each had an extended family, of which his was by far the smallest and the humblest. He kept in touch with his three married sisters with their non-conformist leanings, and remembered them in his will. Visiting Ann's family involved trips to Windsor Castle and Eton College, as well as London rectories at St Stephen's, Wallbrook, and St Benet's Fink. Equally, the London family found Quainton a place of refreshment outside the city. On 23 April, 1711, Charles Stonestreet, Ann's nephew, was baptised at Quainton.

Benjamin and Ann's own family eventually consisted of:

Nathaniel Ingelo: Benjamin's stepson, schooled at Eton and Cambridge and eventually appointed to a college living, Piddlehinton, Dorset. He died unmarried leaving a somewhat twisted and bitter will, virtually accusing his family of tricking him out of his inheritance and not caring for him. It looks like the stepson experience was not a happy one for him.

Ann: 1693–1700, named after her mother. Buried at Quainton.

Winwood: 1695–1701, named after the Winwood family, to whom they would ever be grateful. Buried at Quainton.

Benjamin: 1696–1767 named after his father, schooled at Eton and King's Cambridge. He spent his life as rector of Stower Provost, Dorset, another Eton living. He married his first cousin Katherine Stonestreet in St Paul's Cathedral, and they had a daughter described as "lunatic". Were the storyline to have descended through this Benjamin, it would have been very thin indeed, since Stower Provost experienced little change or drama in his lifetime!

George: 1699–1700, named no doubt after his illustrious grandfather and who lived for only a year, outlived by his grandfather. Buried in Quainton.

Gilbert Edward: 1700–1747, who was a bachelor physician of Bath, apparently stereotypical of the doctors who gathered round the ailing rich who settled in Bath for the waters and the physicians. He seems to have died in Dorchester, where he had a memorial tablet in the parish church. The name Edward recalls his grandfather.

Thomas: 1703–67, named after his uncle, Thomas Evans. He was the youngest son, through whom the storyline continues.

The loss of three young children may not have been unusual for the times, but each must have brought its heartache to the family. Maybe, too, it endeared the village people to their rector and his wife in their sorrow. Their three surviving children were all boys, and all went to Cambridge. Two of them were to become clergy, and Gilbert Edward a medical doctor. This was probably the first Archer generation to have the money and the backing to educate all their children, marking a turning point in the fortunes of the family. Gilbert was educated at Thame and Westminster, Benjamin and Thomas at Eton. Thomas, the favoured youngest, was privileged to have his uncle Thomas Evans, fellow of Eton, as his godfather, as well as Lettice Pigott as his godmother, of whom more anon.

The daily life of a parson in these settled times was fairly predictable, although interesting incidentals appear in the surviving churchwardens' accounts for Quainton.[9] The wardens were overseeing work on the highway in the 1720s. Mr Archer and the wardens met at the Parsonage House to discuss "Thos. Pigott's legacy for putting Poor children to Prentice". The church wall required more dung; the Church Bible required rebinding and this meant sending it to London; at the same time, the church purchased a new Book of Common Prayer. There were some unusual payments to people passing through: nine soldiers with a certificate of being slaves, 1s; paid to several travelling seamen that had great losses and wounded soldiers in the year past £1.7.8; a man that had losses by thunder and lightning; given to a poor woman that came from Turkey 6d; given to eight slaves from Turkey 18 shillings. These hand-outs portray a fluid and unsettled underclass moving round the country surviving on parochial charity.

Another window into the parish comes from the 1709 Visitation of Buckingham. All was in order except the number of unconfirmed adults; there were 120 families, 400–500 souls. There were 200 communicants, of whom 80 had received communion at Easter. There were a few Anabaptists, but they met informally without a Meeting

House. Richard Winwood's almshouses had 17 governors, and the rector was always one of these. There was an endowment of £17 a year to teach 20 poor children to read, and the rector supervised the running of their school. There are a number of charitable persons who teach girls to read, knit, and make lace. Divine service was regularly said. In the winter Sunday afternoons, catechising replaced the sermon.

In 1723, Ann's name appears in a list of landowners who were ordered to take an Oath of Allegiance to the crown: "Anne Archer, wife of Benjamin". The land was presumably her jointure estate near Swindon. At her remarriage, it would have become Benjamin's property legally, but characteristically she still took the oath for it.

An unexpected insight into Benjamin's ministry at Quainton and a pen-portrait of Benjamin himself, comes from a book published in 1741:

> *Memorials and Characters together with the lives of divers Eminent and Worthy persons... collected and compiled from 150 different authors, several scarce pieces and some original Manuscripts, communicated to the Editor... published for John Wilford at the three Flower de Luces in the Old Bailey.*

An "anonymous" author supplied the piece on Lettice Pigott, late of Doddershall in the parish of Quainton. This lady was a childless widow, dead some considerable time, but whose life and works continued to inspire. The author cites her life of prayer, whereby several parts of the day were allotted for her private devotions. He admires her zeal for the Church of England, and tells how she never failed to make the two-mile journey to the church each Christmas Day, even in thick snow. In church, her reverence – especially as she received the sacrament – struck many, including Anon. He also remembered that when the pulpit cloth was stolen in 1709, she replaced it with a new one in crimson velvet with a cushion to match, both decorated with gold trimming. This strikes us as a detail that a six-year-old child would remember.

There are several paragraphs on her role as godmother, for apparently she had many godchildren. She was very generous to them all and steered them towards confirmation; indeed, she presented them with a Book of Instructions to prepare them for confirmation. The author bemoans how few godparents take their role seriously, regarding it merely as a matter of form and civility.

Turning to her attitude to the clergy, Anon observed that she treated them with respect and dignity. "She was far from thinking the Presence of a Clergyman a Kind of Shade, or damp to splendid and elegant Entertainments." Indeed, the clergyman was "a Preservative and Encouragement" of the social life of Doddershall. For 40 years there passed between the Reverend Mr Archer and the good lady "all the good offices becoming the relation of pastor and parishioner". The author goes as far as to say it was a good thing Benjamin died first, because he doubts if he could have withstood the shock of her death! The eulogy concludes by extolling her charitable giving in great detail. The poor of Quainton certainly had a generous benefactor who took a personal interest in their lives. Undoubtedly, the partnership between the minister and chief lady of the parish was to their mutual benefit, as well as that of the parish.

The anonymous author is not hard to trace. The first clue is that Wilford published his book on the basis of subscriptions from the nobility, gentry, and clergy, who paid for its production. Amongst the subscribers from the clergy is the name of the Revd. Thomas Archer! The other clue is in the will of Lettice Pigott, which names at least some of her godchildren including Thomas Archer, who receives £20 from her, as do both his father Benjamin and mother Ann. Everything points to the writer being the youngest Archer son, Thomas, looking back on his upbringing in the rectory at Quainton, and giving a wealth of detail about parish life from one who saw it all for himself.

Although Benjamin was now centred on family life and his parish, old acquaintances still contacted him. Anthony Wood, with his everlasting interest in people and how they relate, wrote to him on 12 April, 1694, enquiring about a recent neighbour of his, Charles Gataker of Hoggeston. It may have been coincidence but Gataker, too, had been the conforming son of an ejected minister. Indeed, the two fathers probably knew each other, since Thomas Gataker had been a member of the Westminster Assembly.

The world moves on and new intellectual questions about old convictions arise in each generation, many never resolved. When it came to science, however, the chances of finding answers by diligent observation increased. The Royal Society had been formed at the Restoration and was pioneering many new insights. A country parson with a university background would have been fascinated by their discoveries, and in Benjamin's case anxious to join in the debate, even as a humble questioner and local practitioner. His particular fascination was fossils, and it was about these that he wrote to Sir Hans Sloane, who was the current secretary of the Royal Society. As well as some revealing correspondence, Benjamin sent specimens to Sloane, at some personal cost as they were no small items – pieces of rock that were thrown up in Quainton quarry, spotted by the eagle-eyed parson and packed up for the metropolis.

There are two letters from Benjamin Archer to Sir Hans Sloane now preserved in the British Library.[10] Unfortunately, neither is dated, and therefore they could have been sent at any time in Benjamin's 40 years in Quainton. So, we cannot pin down the exact time Benjamin began to wrestle with the modern scientific thinking of the time. Of the two letters preserved in the Sloane collection, letter 286 is obviously not the first, since he is enquiring whether Sloane has received the box of stones he had sent from Quainton Hill.

There is a boyish enthusiasm about Benjamin's character that appears again in this correspondence. Benjamin eagerly offers to send more, but has to confess that they would be the same type as before. But he is hungry to know whether Sloane or his friends had seen similar stones. He goes on to say that he has seen a chalk pit near Reading where, in a vein of sand, oysters can be seen. How did these sea fossils get there? Are they relics of the Flood? This was the standard explanation of fossils that was believed to be compatible with the Bible. But Benjamin expresses his uncertainty about this, and in doing so shows that he is moving into a modern scientific view, even though it appears to challenge established religious belief. He acknowledges Sloane's superior knowledge and ironically describes himself as an infidel in these matters, yet one who is willing to become Sloane's Proselyte, thirsty for up-to-date information.

Two hundred and eighty-eight is a more practical letter:

> *According to my promise I have at last left you a box of fossils with a specimen of whatever the parish affords. I confess I knew not how to direct them to your house at Hereford so sent them by my old acquaintance Mr Colly who I hope will see them conveyed to you.*

He then expresses his anxiety about them crumbling and the costs of transport, for some are large and heavy! He had found a cockle, but alas it got left out in the frost and crumbled.

> *If you please to draw with your pen ye figure of any stonework you will have, let it be upon a piece of paper which I may give to the stone diggers and in a little while they will help me find it for you.*

James Archer's patron
John de Critz – Berger Collection: id #5 (Denver, Colorado)
William Parker, 4th Baron Monteagle and 11th Baron Morley. Oil on Panel.
41 x 32 in (104.1 x 84.3 cm)

Dr Syntax was a fictitious cartoon character created by Thomas Rowlandson in the early 1800's. Like his contemporary Thomas Archer, Syntax was an avid follower of the horses

All the Archers appear to have been passionate preachers

St Sepulchres Cambridge where James served his title, known today as the Round Church

St Ethelbugas church and schoolhouse, Yardley where James Archer worked and his son Edward learned. Copyright Geoff Pick and licensed for reuse under the creative common licence. SP1386 Geograph.org.uk

Sawbridgeworth Church where James Archer was brought up and the Leventhorpes worshipped

George & Dragon, Church End, Foulness where Thomas Archer Jnr.
is reputed to have taken on the local wrestlers

Quainton Church (Photo, Jim Gorringe)

The Baptism Register of Yardley with Edward's name and James' signature

A more Exact and Perfect

RELATION

OF THE

Treachery, Apprehension, Conviction, Condemnation, Confession, and Execution,

OF

Francis Pitt, Aged 65.

Who was Executed in *Smithfield* on Saturday,
October the 12. 1644. For endeavouring to betray
the Garrison of *RUSHALL-HALL* in the
County of *Stafford*, to the Enemy.

Published by { *Ithiel Smart* and *Edward Archer*, } two Ministers.

Who were acquainted with him in his life,

and present with him at his death.

By ſpeciall Command

I Corinth. 10. 11. *Now all these things hapned unto them for ensamples, and they are written for our admonition, upon whom the ends of the world are come.*
Verse 12. *Wherefore let him that thinketh he standeth, take heed lest he fall.*
Matth. 26. 41. *Watch and pray, that ye enter not into temptation.*
Prov. 1. 10. *My son, if sinners entice thee, consent thou not.*
Rom. 6. 21. *What fruit have ye in those things, whereof ye are now ashamed.: for the end of those things is death.*
Verse 23. *The wages of sin is death, but the gift of God is eternall life, through Jesus Christ our Lord.*

London, Printed for *John Field*.   *Octob.* 18. 1644.

RE-PRINTED BY W. HENRY ROBINSON, WALSALL.   MARCH, 1881.

Civil War Tract written by Edward Archer

St. Martin's Ludgate where Thomas Archer senior served.
By kind permission of Bob Speel

No 17th century correspondence would be complete without some name-dropping, so: *"I remember well you were a person the Duke of Montagu had a great respect for."* This may be pure affectation, but Benjamin may also want to ensure he is taken seriously. Montagu is now the patron of Quainton, so Benjamin says in effect – as we're both known to the duke, we are equals, even though you have the scientific knowledge! Maybe it was Montagu who had suggested sending Quainton specimens to Sloane.

Since clergy only held their livings during their lifetimes, it is not surprising that they would look for the opportunity to buy property as an investment and an insurance for their families. Benjamin had not inherited any property from either his father or grandfather, so his first experience of owning anything was when he married Ann Evans, who brought Westcott farm near Swindon into the family as her jointure. Ann herself could not own the farm outright as a married woman, but its income would always provide for her throughout her lifetime. The jointure came from her first husband, Nathaniel Ingelo, by whom her son Nathaniel also inherited Ingelo property: Prickwick Farm in Chew Magna. In 1712, Benjamin Archer bought this from his stepson for £600. Nathaniel's own will of 1751 expresses his regret at having sold the family estate and hints that his stepfather, wanting the property for his own sons, put some pressure on him at a time of vulnerability. The only other interest Benjamin had some claim upon was the parish church at Hitcham, where Ann's father had been the rector. The advowson had passed to Ann's brother, Dr Thomas Evans – an unmarried fellow of Eton – who hedged his bets in promising it to the Archer family in perpetuity on the understanding that Eton College actually made the appointments. It took the next 100 years to unravel the confusion!

Benjamin made his will in 1724 when he was 72, although he lived another eight years. It is one of those satisfactory wills that reveals much about the character of the person and his relationships, as well as plenty of practical information. There is the expected puritan commendation of his soul to God with several lines of piety and theology. Incidentally, Benjamin wrote his will himself and did not have the inhibitions of another person listening and scribing. A major concern soon appears in the will:

> *"And now to prevent all false and scandalous reports which may be raised and spread after my decease I think it may be proper and necessary for me to make this serious and solemn protestation that as I have lived so I desire and resolve to dye in the communion of the Church of England and humbly beg God the Father of mercies to preserve this church as it is now established by law in peace truth and godliness evermore."*

Later in the will comes an equally emphatic paragraph that is surely related to Benjamin's overall state of mind as he contemplates not just death but the possibility of his private thoughts and papers becoming public property. He refers to his "books, papers and sermon notes" locked in a desk on his study table, and indeed "all other sermon notes", requesting his wife *"that as she loves me she would take them all with her own hands and commit them to the flames that they may not be read or seen by my sons or any other person how nearsoever related to me"*.

So why should there be rumours about Benjamin dying outside the faith of the Church of England, and why should he be so emphatic about his writings being destroyed? After all, he had been ordained into the church, and ministered first as a college fellow and later as a parish minister for all his working life. Yet, facing death he looked back critically upon his life. He had been brought up in a non-conformist household and his father had been ejected. He had been a risqué young preacher, and no doubt aired views he had since abandoned. He recalled the turmoil of the clash with the bishop and all he might have said and preached in the heat of the moment. Then he had married the daughter of a man who was first ordained as a presbyterian, and whose first husband came from Quaker stock. His sisters retained their non-conformist preferences and one had married another ejected minister. Benjamin retained his friendship with many who continued to move in informal puritan circles. Consequently, contradictions and questions churned away in Benjamin and fed into his teaching and preaching.

Perhaps Benjamin's papers showed how much he may have sympathised with dissent and questioned the orthodoxy of the established church. Now, as he thought of death and legacy, this was not the image he wished to be remembered by. Knowing the pain of his own torn loyalties, as did so many survivors of the Civil War, he did not wish to impose his doubts and questions upon his sons, who were happily serving in the restored Church of England.

There is a touch of paranoia in his efforts to ensure that his writings are destroyed. But there is a paradox about the attention he drew to them by his dramatic request that they should be burned. Why did he not collect all the suspect material himself and dispose of it before he died? Why raise his sons' curiosity and posterity's speculations? Did he feel these sermons were too much part of his story for him to destroy them himself, so that until he died they were there for him to feel and touch; tangible evidences of his pilgrimage? Or was he simply a dramatic character who planted intrigue into his last testament, as he had into his life?

The remainder of his will was more practical: the Chew Magna farm he had purchased from his stepson was to be divided between his other three sons. Ann retained her jointure farm for her continued support, and was also given the household goods and the chaise from the rectory. Gilbert Edward, the doctor son, had the income from the Hitcham advowson, and the parson sons were to divide their father's books "in my outward and forward study". Dr Evans of Eton was to make the division unless Benjamin got round to it in his lifetime. He expressed his concerns that his sons should not fall out over books, property, or money – no doubt he had witnessed all too many such family disputes amongst his parishioners and friends.

Dr Evans journeyed from Eton to take Benjamin's funeral, and died himself within the year. Benjamin was the only Archer to have a memorial plaque inside a church, but in later days it was moved to the exterior wall where the lettering has now worn beyond recognition. Fortunately, a record was made before this loss.[11] Benjamin's memorial is the most elaborate of the five Archers. Neither James nor Edward have known graves, Thomas senior's grave has disappeared, and Thomas junior left a simple inscription. Given that this is the case, we will give Benjamin's memorial in its full Latin glory!

In spe Beatae Resurrectionis, quiescit Infra hunc Tumulum sua cura sibi suisq; dum apud vivos fuit extructum [inter charos at heu! brevis aevi Liberos annam Winwoodum Georgium]

Benjamin Archer S.T.B. Hujus Ecclesiae per quadraginta annos Rector Qualis fuerat Hodierni Viciniam consulant, Priam, omnibus indicabit Supremus Dies. Anna Uxor fidelis, moesta defuncti, Vidus nec non Filii quotquot sunt superstites Benjamin, Gilbertus-Edwardus, Thomas, optime de semeriti nunquam immemores nunquam satis memores future Pietatis et Officii ergo. Hanc qualemcumq; Tabulam communiter posuerint.

Obdormivit in Christo xx Die Augusti annon Salutis MDCCXXXII Aetatis suae LXXXI

The memorial is, of course, the work of his surviving family and is indeed quite simple compared with many 18th century inscriptions. Theologically, too, it is not ambitious. Basically, he died in Christ in the hope of the Resurrection. The day of judgement will reveal his true character, although ask anyone who knew him about the worthiness of that character. His children, departed and living, are all remembered. Priam is a mystery!

Sources

Parish Registers of Newington and Quainton

The History and Antiquities of the County of Buckingham, George Lipscomb MD, 1847

A History of Quainton, Laurie Cooper, 1998

CCEd has details of Benjamin's deaconing and priesting; his appointment to Wexham and Quainton.

Notes

1. Parish registers St Giles, Newington
2. Berkshire Record Office D/A1/174/61
3. *Register of the rectors & fellows, scholars, exhibitioners & Bible clerks of Exeter College, Oxford* by Charles William Boase, 1879. Includes bibliographical references and index.
4. CCEd and Oldfield's *History of Oxford Clerics*
5. *The Life and Times of Anthony Wood* 3.67
6. CCEd
7. Strickland is extensively quoted by Boase (*see* note 3).
8. *The Life and Times of Anthony Wood* 3.337
9. *Buckinghamshire Archaeological Society Records* 12 29-46
10. Sloane Mss 4057 f.286/8 British Library
11. George Lipscomb, *The History and antiquities of the County of Buckingham*, 1847

Thomas Archer Senior (1703–1767): Fourth Generation

Thomas was the youngest son of Benjamin and Ann Archer. His father was 50 and his mother 45 at his birth. He was baptised in his father's church at Quainton on 30 June, 1703. Two of his godparents were his Uncle Thomas, who taught at Eton and after whom he was presumably named, and Lettice Pigott, a godly widow living in Doddershall, a local estate. The account of Benjamin's ministry at Quainton, written by Thomas, included a glittering appreciation of her support for her godchildren, including her role in bringing them to confirmation. When Lettice died in 1720, she left Thomas a small financial legacy and treasured memories of her role as a godmother.[1]

Thomas had two older brothers and a much older stepbrother. There had been other children, but they had died young before Thomas was born. Both his brothers were sent away to school at a young age – Benjamin to Eton, and Gilbert Edward to Thame and later Westminster. But there is no record of Thomas going to boarding school until he was 14. It seems likely that, until then, his father tutored him at home. In the holidays, the rectory must have been a noisy place with four adolescent boys at home, but in school-time a quiet must have descended and Thomas would have felt like an only child.

There were many relatives on both sides of the family but only Ann's appear in the historic record as visitors to Quainton. Her father, Canon George Evans of Windsor, had died before Thomas was born, but his wife Rebecca lived until 1712 when Thomas was nine, so he would have known her and probably visited her in her grace-and-favour residence at Windsor Castle. It would have been a secure childhood, with a sense of being rooted in important circles.

Thomas was not sent to Eton until he was 14, by which time his brother Benjamin was at Merton College, Oxford, and Gilbert Edward was at St John's, Cambridge. Maybe Benjamin and Ann found it hard to relinquish their youngest son any earlier. Thomas soon joined his brothers at university, matriculating in 1721 at Merton, Oxford, where he also obtained his BA. For his MA, he migrated to King's, Cambridge, a college with historic links to Eton.

It is unclear why he was ordained as a deacon in Chichester. At 24, he was slightly under age when the ordination took place in the Bishop's Palace at Chichester on 11 July, 1727, conducted by Bishop Edward Waddington, who had recently restored the crumbling old palace. The clue may be that Waddington was an old Etonian himself, had become a fellow in 1720, and probably met the teenage Thomas at that time, seeing him as a potential ordinand whom he could encourage and personally ordain in his newly-restored chapel. The old-Etonian network was ubiquitous then as now, although scholarship and the church were the spheres that Eton then specialised in.

Thomas's stepbrother, Nathaniel Ingelo, received the Eton living of Piddlehinton in 1726, and stayed there all his life. His brother Benjamin received another Eton living, Stower Provost. Both were tiny and sleepy West Country livings. Thomas, too, could have spent his life in a small Eton living, had not circumstances intervened.

Meanwhile, it was two years before he was priested, this time in a more conventional setting in Christ Church Cathedral, Oxford, by Bishop John Potter. With his MA in hand, he was now ready for a parish, and once again Providence smiled and his luck was in! Richard Sleech, Rector of Hitcham, dropped dead. The living was in the hands of Thomas's godfather, Uncle Thomas Evans, who had received the advowson from his father, Canon George Evans, young Thomas's grandfather.

Thomas was instituted on All Fools' Day, 1730 by Richard Reynolds, Bishop of Lincoln; the Lincoln Diocese at that time reached right down to the Thames. The same year, his brother Benjamin was installed at Stower Provost and Tober. Both were tiny parishes, but both brothers added fashionable chaplaincies to their CVs. Benjamin took on the Countess of Winchelsea (not the famous poetess who had died in 1720), and Thomas served the Countess of Orkney and Inchiquin, who lived at nearby Cliveden with her family. Her husband had been MP for Windsor but was now MP for Tamworth. It would have been necessary to have had a certain class about oneself to be a chaplain in a grand country home, and the Archer brothers had the connections and confidence to slip into the role.

Whereas Benjamin was far from London or the universities, Thomas was a stone's throw from Eton and all his connections there, as well as being within easy travelling distance of London and Oxford. Cliveden, now a well-known National Trust house, was a centre of social and aristocratic networking through which he would have been meeting many "important" people. So, the two brothers' lives went in very different directions at this point, although both were to experience their fair share of tragedy in relation to their marriages.

No sooner were the brothers settled than their 80-year-old father died at Quainton. His widow, Ann, came to live with son Thomas at Hitcham, where she had herself grown up and where she chose to be buried near her father. She lived little more than a year after her husband's death, and left a will. To her "dear son Nathaniel" she left £20, perhaps mindful of his lack of recognition in her husband's will. The other three boys were to divide whatever was left of her money and goods between them. Several gold rings were bequeathed to relatives. It was a typically feminine will, in that her sister Mary received her best clothes and her servant Martha the remainder, along with curtains. Most surprising was her request that her body should be opened by a skilled surgeon before burial. Perhaps Dr Gilbert Edward Archer had shared the difficulties medical students had in obtaining bodies. But Ann, too, must have been convinced of the necessity of bodies being made available for research, and unperturbed by the effect of dissection on her ultimate resurrection.

The same year, her brother Thomas also died and he, too, was buried at Hitcham, adding to the growing number of family memorial plaques on the exterior east wall of the church. Clergy families might not possess historic houses, but they did have access to ancient churches that housed memorials for posterity. St.Mary's, Hitcham, was gathering the Archer story to itself. It must have been a secure and comfortable place for Thomas to begin his ministry.

Not surprisingly, there are no significant events to lighten up the story of Hitcham and Thomas's ministry in this tiny parish. In part, he was living the life of a typical gentleman academic, 18th century parson, maintaining his links with Eton and with old Etonians. One of his letters, written in August 1737,[2] has survived in a collection gathered by the old Etonian and antiquarian, William Cole. It was sent from Windsor to Dr Browne Willis of Waddon Hall, Fenny Stratford, Bucks. Willis was another antiquarian, typical of the times with a private income, often spending unlimited time on what could seem trivia but for which historians are nevertheless grateful. He was a collector of books and coins, and established a fun festival in Fenny Stratford on St Martin's Day (11 November), famed for its Fenny Poppers – maybe the original party-popper. But lest we deem him too frivolous, we should remember that he was also the local MP.

Apparently, Thomas went to stay with Willis Browne and discussed a project being worked on which required a full list of the fellows of Eton. Willis's existing list had missing names, as did another list held by Dr Berriman, also a fellow of Eton who was rector of St Andrew's, Undershaft. So, Willis asked Thomas to take on the task of compiling a complete new list. This request opened a window into Thomas's character. Moving in this scholarly circle, did he have the temperament for this fine academic work? He points out to Willis that the truth was that "your Paper is wrote so exceeding thick & close that there is no room to perfect it". Would it not be easier to contact Berriman direct and sort it out between them? He helpfully gives guidance on contacting Berriman: "His time of going to London is Michelmas and at any time between then & Lady Day you are pretty sure of finding him at the parsonage there." And in case that might not work, Thomas has another suggestion. "He tells me Dr Rawlinson too has an account of the Society." Rawlinson was a famous non-juror, a member of the Antiquarian Society, financed from a private income, and in Cole's words "indefatigable in the search of antiquities". Finally, Thomas assumes Willis would not want him to post the list back immediately "supposing you would hardly think it worth double postage".

I think we can safely say that while Thomas was at home in the circle of antiquarians that Eton freely produced, he had no great enthusiasm himself for the hard work involved. This was probably his temperament, but may also be connected with his search for a wife, currently underway.

Now he had a parish, he could properly care for a family, but finding the right lady was a delicate matter. Fortunately, another old Etonian was on hand to help him. The Revd. Dr John Reynolds was from Exeter, where he was the master of the grammar school. He was a published academic who networked widely. In 1729, aged nearly 60, he was ordained privately in the Bishop's Palace, Holborn, by the Bishop of Ely, which opened the way for him becoming a Canon of Exeter and a fellow of Eton.

Reynolds was twice married, and by his second wife had a daughter, Catherine, baptised at St Lawrence's in Exeter on 31 August, 1714. So, in 1738 she was 24, and the family would be concerned to find her a suitable husband. Her father spotted Archer's suitability and availability, so the match was soon forthcoming, having been agreed by both parties. Neither was rich, but both had status and Thomas had prospects. The couple were granted a licence to wed by the Faculty Office on 29 December, 1738. The newlyweds had every expectation of a long and happy family life. Catherine's cousin was to become the famous Sir Joshua Reynolds, but she would not live long enough to benefit from this connection.

As it happened, Thomas's brother Benjamin also tied the knot that year. As befitted the older brother, he married first on 22 August, having chosen his cousin Catherine Stonestreet as his bride. Their marriage was at St Paul's Cathedral, since the Stonestreets were a city clergy family. Neither of Thomas's other two brothers, Nathaniel Ingelo and Gilbert Archer, ever married.

The Hitcham registers for this period are barely legible, but when made out make sober reading. In 1739, there is a private baptism of Catherine's and Thomas's son John, named after Catherine's father. On 6 May, 1740, there are baptism entries for John and Audrey Ann, children of Catherine and Thomas. The premature private baptism suggests that John was a delicate child, and indeed he died before the end of the year. Then on 10 April, 1741, Catherine herself was buried at Hitcham and her daughter did not long survive her, being buried on 6 October, 1741. It seems that Catherine died from complications following childbirth, and the baby Audrey Ann could not be kept alive for long. In three short years Thomas had gone from a joyful newlywed to a widower grieving for his whole family. Hitcham, which had seemed such an idyll, must have now felt like a parish of shadows and sorrow. Maybe it was time to move.

Brother Benjamin fared little better, losing his infant son at birth and his wife in childbirth later. However, his surviving daughter did grow to adulthood, albeit as a woman with mental health problems.

Perhaps as an antidote to this time of tragedy, Thomas was writing his piece on Lettice Pigott and her relationship with his father. Unsurprisingly, he glamorised them both. Lettice was the perfect hostess, treating her parish minister as her personal chaplain with deep respect and an openness that some might deem over-familiar. Yet both parties knew just where to draw the line and retain those boundaries that the Pigotts' wealth and status required in contemporary society. Above all, their bond was spiritual and based on their mutual faith and commitment to the church they both loved – Holy Cross and

St Mary, Quainton, bastion of the values and sufficiency of the Church of England. Writing up this account must have helped Thomas centre himself afresh and look to his own future as a priest in that church.

Undoubtedly, a bigger parish and a more vibrant milieu would help him to rebuild his life. The Bishop of London, Edmund Gibson, appears in history as a churchman who was wise and respected. However, he was not above using his office to seek a living for his own nephew, named after him. Thomas found that he held a trump card in making a deal with the bishop – the living of Hitcham. Although it was still unclear exactly how the advowson was to operate from the terms of Thomas Evans's will, Thomas Archer would be able to tell the bishop that it was in some ways shared between Eton and his older brother Benjamin. This seemed just the sort of living that the bishop was looking for to present his nephew.

In turn, he offered Thomas the living of Finchley, which was substantial but not special. So, he threw in St Martin's, Ludgate, in the city and worth more than Finchley. And seeing he was going to be that near St Paul's, how about a prebendary's stall? Rugemere was currently vacant, and to round off the deal Thomas would be a Reader in divinity and his licence would allow him to be a preacher throughout London.

There was a problem in that Thomas would technically have two parishes and therefore be a pluralist. However, there were ways of dealing with this and the judicious *Acts of the Archbishop* included a dispensation on the grounds that the joint income was no more than £300 and the parishes were only six miles apart.[3]

The appointments duly appeared in the *Gentleman's Magazine,* and Thomas was instituted as rector of Finchley on 30 September and St Martin's, Ludgate, on 12 October, 1743. Only then did he formally resign from Hitcham, having negotiated with his brother and Henry Bland, the provost of Eton, young Gibson's appointment to Hitcham, the registers tactfully naming Benjamin Archer and Henry Bland as joint patrons.

The self-same Henry Bland was also dean of Durham and had earlier conducted a glamorous wedding at Eton on 8 November, 1740. The *Weekly Miscellany* reported it: *"On Tuesday last was married at Eton by the Rev. Dr Bland Dean of Durham, Mr. John Carter, an eminent bookseller near the Royal Exchange, to Miss Dixon daughter of Mrs Dixon, housekeeper to the Rt. Hon. Sir Robert Walpole at Houghton, a young lady of great beauty, merit and fortune."*[4]

As well as dean of Durham and provost of Eton, Bland was also rector of two small churches on the Walpole estate in Norfolk. He is referred to by contemporaries as "a great favourite of Walpole". Bland and Walpole had both been boys at Eton in their youth, and Bland had accordingly benefited from the connection. John Carter was the nephew of another Eton fellow, Dr Carter. So, the scenario would be something like this: Bland, visiting Houghton and checking on his churches, met the charming housekeeper's daughter, Mary Dixon. He mentioned her back at Eton, and Dr Carter pricked up his ears since he was looking for a suitable bride for his nephew. The marriage was agreed upon, and arranged with Dr Bland presiding. Almost a fairy tale, except that within two years John Carter had died and Mary returned to her mother at Houghton.

Shortly after his nephew's demise, Dr Carter sensed his own imminent departure. He made his will on 30 November, 1745, appointing three executors, one being Mary Carter, widow, and another Thomas Archer, widower, suggesting that plans were well on the way for their future together. Carter's will was proved on 7 January, 1746, and Mary and Thomas's wedding followed some six months later on 23 June at Great Bircham parish church on the Walpole estate in Norfolk. There is no record of who took it, but since the rector was Dr Henry Bland it seems likely that he presided over Mary's second wedding as he had over her first one. Presumably Mary remained a lady of great beauty, merit, and fortune. Indeed, her fortune had increased considerably, since her first husband's will left everything to her with a simple request that she looked after his relatives in their times of need.

Mary's background in Norfolk and Houghton meant that Thomas was catapulted into fashionable Norfolk circles by his marriage. The famous clerical diary of the Norfolk parson, James Woodforde, makes frequent mention of the Bodham family with whom Woodforde often used to dine, enjoying those gargantuan portions he unashamedly describes in the diary. Whilst he does not himself mention meeting the Archers, Thomas Bodham's aunt Susannah was a close friend of Thomas and Mary Archer, who are accorded a few glowing lines of gratitude in her will. Gentry circles were amazingly interlaced.

So, Thomas settled into a life divided between his two busy parishes. St Martin's boasted a Wren church built a little over 50 years earlier, and the churchwardens' accounts paint a rich picture of the church. Apart from its architecture, the church was adorned with red velvet cushions and altar frontals fringed with gold tassels, and damask tablecloths and napkins. It also boasted a large fire engine with 30 yards of leather pipe, which was periodically called into service in the parish.

Thomas had a parsonage dwelling in Holiday Yard for his times of residence in the parish. James Boswell, the diarist, visited the church on 15 May, 1763 although we do not know whether Thomas or a curate took the service. Boswell was impressed: "I attended Divine service in Ludgate church with patience and thanksgiving and was much edified."

The churchwardens' accounts for St Martin's show just how busy a parish it was. Orphans were put into homes; poor people were provided with decent burials; the sick were sent to hospital; papists were hunted down; sexton and organ blower were paid; candles and glass lanthorns for the church were regularly ordered. Repairs to church property, as well as to the church itself, were organised; water was provided for houses owned by the church; the vestry chimney was swept; a workhouse was overseen; and the placing of apprentices was undertaken. Ascension Day saw a parish feast day, with cakes provided for all. On Christmas

Day, Thomas received 10 shillings for his sermon.

Most striking of all is the list of soldiers' wives who received money from the parish and are named in the accounts. In 1745, there were more than 1000. In 1750, eight poor sailors taken by the Algerians, some without tongues, each received four shillings. Of course, Thomas himself was not responsible for the daily complex administration of the parish, but he was responsible overall for seeing the system was maintained and the churchwardens were up to their tasks. His name appears occasionally in the accounts throughout his period as rector. Poignantly, the last time is in the year of his death when the wardens were engaged in transferring a local charity to three new trustees, of which he was to be one.

The churchwardens' accounts for Finchley do not exist; references to the fire of 1830 are suggested as the probable reason. There would have been many parallels, however, although Finchley was a country parish in comparison with the buzz of St Martin's, which, quite unlike the parish today, was a highly populated residential area. It appears that Thomas chose the quieter parish for his family life and quiet study. So, the Archers lived in their spacious rectory at Finchley, surrounded by pictures and books.

Thomas's library there merits a study of its own, and a list of some of its books is appended to this chapter. When it was auctioned in 1768, it numbered some 4,000 items ,with the addition of his brother Benjamin's collection, bequeathed to him shortly before. Volumes dated from the 16th century to the year he died, for he was adding books to it until the end of his life. This was a coming together of the Archers' ancestral library, with books published as far back as the Reformation. The sale was held on 1 February, 1768, at P. Shropshire's, the King's Arms, and Golden Ball, New Bond Street. The full contents of the library can still be read in *A List of Catalogues of English Book Sales 1676–1900*, held in the British Library.

Clerical libraries are windows into clergy thinking. In this case, it is unclear whether Thomas or Benjamin had bought the many 18th century books, although Thomas seems the likelier candidate from his living amongst intellectual stimulation in the capital. A book does not necessarily tell us of someone's views – they may have bought it to argue against it. The Archer library had many old sermons and a deal of puritan writings, but these seem to flow into more mainstream and even high church thought, with novels, history, travel and science well represented.[5]

In the ambience of such a library, it was natural for Thomas to do some theological study, so whilst his wife was pregnant he painstakingly edited and published a volume of sermons by Revd. Nathaniel Marshall from original manuscripts.[6] This was not a commercial venture, being paid for by Marshall's widow, who probably lived in the parish since her husband had been rector of Finchley shortly before Thomas. Which raises the question of why Thomas undertook this task at this time. Was it a favour to his predecessor's widow? Did he particularly admire Marshall, and does this give us some idea of Thomas's theology? In his preface to the sermons, which he dated 8 November, 1749, he boldly asks the question whether there are not already sufficient sermons published. In his justification for yet another volume, he quotes Dean Sherlock: *"Men of different capacities and palates, who in such a variety may meet both with what will please and do them good."*

Thomas admits that some sermons date quickly, but then argues that Marshall employed all the politeness and engagement of language (of which he was an uncommon master) in the service and maintenance of Gospel principles and religious morals. Above all, Marshall stood out for having gone *"deep into the study of the Primitive writers early in life",* and far from making him incomprehensible, his acquaintance with the Fathers added to his being *"a popular and eminent preacher".* Marshall was squarely in the Reformation tradition, seeing the roots of the Church of England in the ancient church from which the Roman church had strayed. In particular, he had translated the writings of St Cyprian for his generation. His writings on the relationship of church and state were considered to be less scholarly than pragmatic; he was, after all, a king's chaplain and his sermons were dedicated to the Queen. So, Thomas's task was to highlight the work of a scholarly and conservative man in mind and character, who maintained a lofty view of the Church of England. And in doing so we see Thomas himself reflected in this scholarly preacher, sermonising along similar lines himself, proclaiming Gospel principles and religious morals.

It is significant that although Thomas's life runs parallel with that of John Wesley, there is no surviving record of any contact with the Methodist movement. Grandfather Edward would surely have thrilled to the preaching of Wesley and Whitfield, but Thomas was the product of scholarship and gentrification, affirming the Gospel quietly and with dignity within the safety of the parish system.

There is little doubt that Thomas was a conscientious parish priest, resident in Finchley and active at St Martin's, Ludgate. Throughout his ministry, he had at least one curate licensed to Finchley, giving him flexibility in serving both parishes. He would have paid his curates from his stipends. The rectory would have been a quiet haven for study and hospitality, cared for by servants. There would have been trips by coach to Norfolk to meet Mary's family and maintain other friendships.

All seemed steady in the Archer household, except that the lack of any children left a gap. Yet that, too, was remedied in 1750 by the birth of their son, Thomas. Young Thomas was baptised on 19 February at St Leonard's, Foster Lane, in the shadow of St Paul's. The vicar, Richard Bullock, was a near contemporary at Eton of Thomas, the father, and may well have taken the baptism. Thomas proved to be an only child, whether for medical, emotional or other reasons remains unknown. One godfather was his uncle, Benjamin, and another could have been Thomas Stonestreet. According to his ordination papers, he was educated at home by his father, which, for an only child, may have been a somewhat lonely experience.

Later in the year of Thomas's baptism, Mary's new stepfather, Ambrose Payne, died at Houghton where he had been Walpole's steward for many years. Thomas Archer was a witness of his will, and must have been visiting Houghton at this time. Indeed, the Archers would have been frequent visitors to this great house in Norfolk where Mary had been brought up and her mother was still the housekeeper. To be this close to the "Prime Minister" would have given them status and reflected glory. Yet lest they grew too grand, it would have been noted, they were not nobility and their connection to Houghton was in fact through high-class servants.

In 1752, the date of the New Year changed to 31 December and September 2 to 14 were written off, to the consternation of many souls who thought their lives were being shortened. No doubt the rector of Finchley had soothing things to say to his disgruntled flock about this.

In 1755, the living descendants of Thomas's grandfather, Canon George Evans, got together to divide up their inheritance by effectively cashing in the land Evans had purchased around Hitcham.[7] These legal papers provide an overview of the social situation of this generation of Archers. The two Archer brothers were clergy in Dorset and London, and Dr Gilbert Edward was dead. The Stonestreet cousins – George, Nicholas, and Rebecca – were all unmarried and lived together in comfort in houses in Cross Street, Islington. The men had all been East India Company traders who made money and retired early, able to call themselves *gent* without compunction. Another set of cousins were in Dorset, and currently Philip Mountague was rector of the Eton living of Piddlehinton. Philip was unmarried but his sister wed another clergyman, William Baker, a Somerset cleric.

The other place we can look to see the social grouping that Thomas felt most bound to, is his will:

Brother Benjamin: five guineas (which he would never receive, since he died before his brother).

Cousins Mountague and Stonestreet: four guineas each.

Robert Parr, Rector of Horsted, Norfolk: two guineas. A contemporary at Eton and an academic.

Mrs Susanna Bodham, clergy widow of Swaffham, Norfolk: one guinea.

His curates at St Martin's and Finchley: one guinea each.

Dr William Dodwell of White Waltham: one guinea. Dodwell was a prolific writer and protagonist for Christian orthodoxy.

Thus, this fourth generation of Archers saw an ascent in social standing for the family, but not a rise into the higher echelons of the clergy. Everything about Thomas's life was comfortable, beginning with his upbringing in the vicarage at Quainton. It was his mother's family who helped raise the status of the Archers, especially Ann's brother Thomas, who was a lifelong fellow of Eton. It was this Thomas who made it possible for his nephew and godson to join him at the school, along with his brother Benjamin and more distant Palmer cousins.

Eton may not have had the social status that it has today, but it was on its way to that position, especially since Robert Walpole had been a pupil there. What it did have in abundance was connections: both the families of other pupils, and those of the staff. It was these connections that provided Thomas with both his wives, the second one bringing him into a new social circle in Norfolk around the home of Walpole at Houghton. Thomas's friends remained parish clergy, albeit academics with Eton and Cambridge connections.

Thomas was probably richer than his predecessors, but still his worldly estate was modest. Most of his possessions came to him through his marriage to Mary Carter, who herself had received property from her Dixon and Shuckforth roots, as well as her first husband. Thomas himself came into a cash inheritance when the Evans estate was sold off in 1755. All this passed to his widow at his death, presumably with the unstated understanding that she would pass it to her son, 17-year-old Thomas, now at Trinity College, Cambridge, when he came of age. Mary's brother, Francis Dixon, had also done well from the Walpole connection, and had been appointed Receiver General of Cambridge. Did Thomas presume he need not set up the usual trustees as custodians of his wife's affairs, since her brother was more than capable of helping her to manage them herself? It may have been a practical position, but it was to go horribly wrong.

Thomas died in 1767, and in his will left money for the poor of Finchley and Ludgate, and committed himself to God in the traditional formula of the Prayer Book and his forebears. He trusted not in works or wealth but only in the merits and death of the Son of God. In an age when people began to question this orthodoxy and indeed become more secular, he did not deviate from the faith that had been handed down to him. His closest friends were academics, most with a background at Eton, and all impeccably orthodox with a much higher view of the institutional church than his forebears. Yet like his father, he was above all a conscientious parish priest who also loved his study and his books.

Thomas requested that he should be buried at Hitcham close to his mother, first wife, and infant children, and alongside the memorials of his ancestors and other members of his mother's family. In spite of the sadness of his Hitcham days, the ancestral connection pulled him back there so that in spite of the inconvenience, his body was transported to Hitcham for burial. His son composed a Latin inscription for his tomb. Neither the grave nor the inscription has survived.

Sources

1. Bucks RO D/A/ WF/80/202
2. Letter to Browne Willis Coles Cambridgeshire 5833.181 [British Library]
3. Acts of the Archbishop 8,245 [Lambeth]
4. The account of Mary Dixon's wedding is to be found in *A dictionary of the printers & booksellers who were at work in England, Scotland & Ireland from 1726–75* (Gen Soc.PR/PRI).
5. *See* the appendix below.
6. Nathaniel Marshall has an entry in the ODNB. The volume Archer edited is *Sermons on Several Occasions, Volume 4. 1750* British Library.
7. Indenture in the Bucks Record Office D678/4

Appendix:
THE ARCHER LIBRARY
built up over the generations

The library of the Revd. Thomas Archer and his brother Benjamin was sold by auction by Walter Shropshire at The Kings Arms and Golden Ball in New Bond Street on 1 February, 1768. From a catalogue in the British Museum 1915 [now in the British Library], there are 4,000+ volumes listed, many being sermons of which I have made a selection. I have also selected the theology and history predominantly:

Tacitus, Opera, 1589
Medici, Artis Princip, 1567
Mathioli, Commentaris in Dioscondam, 1565
Coopers Thesaurus, 1573
Bacon, Omnia Opera, 1665
Paradise Lost, 1736
Chronica del Reg Dom Alonio, 1534
Crudens Concordance, 1761
Baxters Rest, 1653
Sherlock, State of the Socinian Controversy, 1694
Prynne, Antipathy of the English Lordly Prelacy to Regal Monarchy
    and Civil Unity, 1641
Tovey, History and Antiquity of the Jews in England, 1738
Bowers History of the Popes, 1749
Wall, History of Infant Baptism, 1707
Ridley, Life of Bishop Ridley, 1763

Willis, Survey of the Cathedrals, 1727

Lockes Letters concerning Toleration, 1764

Tindal, Christianity as old as Creation, 1739

Whole Duty of a Woman, 1739

Aesop's Fables, 1553

History of Bruce, King of Scotland, 1615

History of William Wallace [Defender of the liberty of the Scots]

A Defence of the Godlie, 1594

Ministers against the Slander of D. Bridges, 1587

A sermon at the Coronation of King James I by the Bishop of
    Winchester, 1603

The description of a true visible Christian, 1599

80 + sermons preached at St Paul's Cross, 1550-1600

Sermon preached by the Bishop of Chichester to the Queen, 1576

Cooke's complete Copyholder, 1694

Littleton 61 sermons, 1680

Allestry, 18 sermons, 1669

Allestry, 41 sermons, 1684

Featly, 70 sermons, 1639

Bishop Hall, Works, 1625

Collection of Cases to recover the Dissenters to the communion of the
    C of E, 1694

Scrivener, Course of Divinity, 1674

Comber, Companion of the Temple, 1688

Chillingworth, The Way to Salvation, 1684

Hakewill, Apology of Power and the Providence of God, 1630

Newcombe, Last Judgement [poem], 1723

Montague, Acts and monuments of the Church before Christ's
    Incarnation, 1642

Hooker, Laws of Ecclesiastical Polity, 1661

Fuller, Pisgah-sight of Palestine, 1650

Field, History of the Church, 1628

Covel, Account of the Greek Church, 1722

Fuller, Church History of Britain, 1655

Walker, Sufferings of the Clergy, 1714

Burnet, History of the Reformation, 1715

Heylen, History of the Reformation, 1674

Heylen, History of Presbyterianism, 1676

Heylen, Life of Archbishop Laud, 1671

Stillingfleet, History of the British Churches, 1685

Newcourt, History of the Diocese of London, 1708

Hacke, Life of Archbishop Williams, 1693

Denton, Tracts of Presbetery, Independency etc., 1685

Fisher, Laud's Conference with the Jesuits, 1673

Malebranche, Search after Truth, 1700

Browne, Description of the Muscles, 1698

Locke, On Human Understanding, 1694

Johnson, Dictionary

Hobbes, Moral and Political Works, 1714-1750

Ingelo, Bentivolo and Urania, 1682

Philips, Don Quixote, 1689

Burton, Anatomy, 1660

Common Place Book[Mss]

King Henry V, Play [Mss]

Spencer, Fairie Queen, 1611

Biblia Hebraica, 1543

Novi testament Catholica exposition, ecclesiastica, 1570

Holy Bible bound in Turkey, gilt leaves, Camb., 1629

Dr Samuel Clarke, Works, 1738

Tillitson, Works, 1728

Smallridge, Sermons, 1729

Works of the author of the Whole Duty of Man, 1709

Taylor, Life of Christ, 1678

Cave, Lives of the Apostles

Cave, Lives of the Primitive Fathers, 1677
Patrick, Lowth and Whitby, Commentary, 1765
Stackhouse, History of the Bible, 1755
Burkit, NT Paraphrases, 1765
Bingham, Works, 1726
Mason, Vindication of the C of E, 1728
Le Neve, Dignitaries, 1716
Leslie, Theological Works, 1721
Wheatley, Illustrations of BCP, 1726
Fiddes, Body of Divinity, 1718
Samuel Johnson, Works, 1713
Spotswood, History of Scotland, 1677
Pearson, Exposition of the Creed, 1704
Burnet, Exposition of the 39 Articles, 1699
Bishop Hacket, Sermons, 1675
Hammond, Paraphrases, 1753
Joseph Mede, Works, 1669
Cudworth, Intellectual System of the Universe, 1678
Burnet, Theory of the Earth, 1697
Campbell, Doctrine of a middle state, 1721
History of China, 1688
Ockley, History of the Saracens, 1757
London Magazine [complete 1732-1767]
Samuel Wesley, Poems, 1742
Watts, Hymns and Poems, 1722/5
Fielding, Joseph Andrews, 1764
Fielding, Pamela
The History and Gallantry of Christiana, Queen of Sweden, 1697
Hume, Philosophical Essay, 1748
Swift, Intelligence, 1730
[And more by Swift]
Moll Flanders, 1753

Pascal, Thoughts on Religion, 1749

History of Bruce, King of Scotland, 1615

History of William Wallace, 1594

A defence of the godlie ministers against the slanders of D. Bridges, 1589

Ross, Views of all the religions in the world, 1696

Sherlock, Future State, 1723

Sale, Koran, 1764

Stillingfleet, Answer to Locke, 1697

Whitfield, Sermons, 1738

Bangorian controversy?

Calamy, Baxter Abridged, 1713

Clarendon, History of the Rebellion, 1712

Barclay, Apology for Quakers, 1736

Bishop's Exposition of the church catechism with large alterations and notes by Dr. [sic] Archer, 1736

Mrs Burnet, Methods of Devotion, 1713

The Clergyman's Intelligencer, a list of patrons, 1745

Clagett, The Operation of the Spirit, 1680

Luther, A very comfortable and necessary sermon, 1570

Ponet, A notable sermon concerning the right use of the Lord's Supper, before the King at Westminster, 1550

A Funeral Oration made the 14th day of June by John Hooper, the year of our salvation, 1549

Domestic or household sermon for a godly house holder to his children and family, compiled by the godly learned man Christopher Hegend …trans by Reginalde. Ipswich, 1548

Symon Mathewe, Sermon made at the Cathedral church of St.Paul, 27 June, 1535

Echard, Miseries of the inferior Clergy, 1722

Fell, The Epistles of St Paul, 1684

Free Thoughts in Defence of a Future State, 1700

Gedde, Church History of Ethiopia, 1696

Gentlemen instructed in a virtuous and happy life, 1713

A Gentleman's Calling, 1677

Grotius, Truth of Christianity, 1683

Hammond, History of the Bible, 1717

Hicks, Letters to and from a Popish priest, 1705

Index to sermons since the Reformation, 1751

Law, A Serious Call, 1732

Methodism – a tract for and against

Mahometism fully explained, 1723

Nichols, Consolation to parents for the death of children, 1701

Peirce, Vindication of the Dissenters, 1718

Penn, tracts, 1756

Indigo Jones, An Account of Stonehenge, 1655

Waters of Bath, 1725

Servants Directory

Health Restored or the Triumph of Nature over Physic, Doctors and
    Apothecaries, 1740

Randall, Semi-Virgilian Husbandry, 1764

PRINTS & DRAWINGS – a selection

Mezzotint of an Indian converted to the Christian religion by Faber;
    full length portrait

Mezzotint of Garrick, Between Tragedy & Comedy by Charles
    Carbutt

By Ms.Ardell – many

Engraving of Joseph and Potiphars wife by Jan Freij

Holy Family by Pittan from Raphael

9 etchings of landscapes by Bartlozzi

Mercury giving Bacchus to the care of the nymphs

Mr. Pelham

General Monkton

Captain Lockhart
Lord Henley
Earl of Chatham, Houston
William, Duke of Cumberland
Jesus bearing the cross, Raphael
Ecco Homo, Van Dyke
6 hunting pieces – Rembrandt
The Four Seasons, Hollar
Drawing of a Goldfinch
The Earl of Chatham, Houron
Miss Lascelles, Watson
Maria Louise des Tassio, Van Dyke
St. Scholastica
A complete microscope in a mahogany cabinet

Also Books on:
Architecture, Antiquities, Maps, Physics, Perspective, Geography,
    Chirurgery, Music, Harmony,
Anatomy, Agriculture, Law, Poetry, Novels, Plays, Astronomy,
    Growing Vegetables

Thomas Archer Junior (1750–1832): Fifth Generation

Thomas Archer junior acknowledged that he had been born into wealth and privilege, which for the earlier part of his life he took for granted. It was, nevertheless, a lonely life as the only child in a rambling London vicarage, where the servants and horses were perhaps his chief playmates. There were cousins: Catherine Archer in Dorset – a delicate child later suffering from mental illness, and children of Uncle Francis Dixon in Upwell, Cambridgeshire. It is unlikely that they were close. There were probably visits to Houghton Hall, where his grandmother remained as housekeeper. Houghton would have opened Thomas's eyes to grand country living.

Nearer his home in Finchley, en route to the city, in Islington, were a host of second cousins from the gentry family of Stonestreet. None of them were married, however, and visiting might not have been a small boy's idea of fun. Three bachelor cousins and their two spinster sisters lived in houses in Cross Street. Thomas Stonestreet might well have been a godfather, since he left "Tommy Archer", as he called him, 50 guineas in his will. He had been a merchant in the Indies, and retired with plenty of money and a houseful of exotic memorabilia. The last surviving Stonestreet was Rebecca, who died in 1794 and whose legacy to Thomas, by then aged 44, was to pay off his debts and leave him a gold mourning ring with an amethyst set in it. She also left provision for the education of Thomas's son. However, the bulk of the Stonestreet fortune went to a distant cousin, on condition that he added Stonestreet to his name.

It may be worth reflecting on the shrinking of gentry families in the 17th century. Many did not marry; single men and women created households from relatives and servants that provided a comfortable and congenial way of life. The growing wealth of gentry families meant that marriage was not necessarily the best option for a comfortable life. This in turn encouraged immorality and illegitimacy. Furthermore, the growing importance of property in gentry marriages, illustrated by the proliferation of marriage settlements, led them closer to the behaviour of the aristocracy where wealth trumped love and could leave both partners emotionally short-changed. Thomas was the product of a love-match, though it is unclear why he was an only child.

He was educated at home, according to his university records. With his father's connections and income, he could surely have been sent to Eton. Perhaps his parents could not face their only son leaving home. Perhaps Thomas senior had memories of Eton that he was later unhappy about. We don't know whether he had a tutor for his son or whether he did all the teaching himself. His extensive library was a resource for any young person hungry for information. The effectiveness of this education was vindicated by Tommy matriculating at Cambridge and becoming a scholar of Trinity at the age of 17.

However, it was not to be an easy start for him. First, in early 1767 his Uncle Benjamin, vicar of the Eton living of Stower Provost, died. Then, more devastating for young Thomas, came the sudden death of his own father that same summer. The one thing Thomas and his mother were left with was money, since everything was left to them. They would need to move from the rectory, and as Thomas was already at Cambridge it made sense for Mary to take a house there for them both. Apparently, Thomas immediately invested in a pack of hounds and ensured he had a top class horse, in order to facilitate his lifelong love of hunting.

Mary Archer now had access to a small fortune, with her various Norfolk properties and all of her husband's money. She was, however, a woman, and with her son being under-age she was expected to take advice from a worldly wise man. No name is mentioned, but the obvious person was her brother, Francis Dixon, who thanks to Walpole's patronage had been one time high sheriff of Cambridge and Hunts and was receiver general of Cambridge. But whether through him or another, the money was lost, and according to her son, Mary died of a broken heart. Her body was taken back to her family home, Saham Toney in Norfolk, where her mother had recently returned after her many years as Walpole's housekeeper. Mary was buried on 23 June, 1772 in the chancel of St George's, and her name was later added to a memorial stone that included precious details about her family story that became a key to unravelling this phase of the Archer family. It is a genealogist's delight, in English, uncluttered with piety or poetry, just pure detailed information about family connections.

> Near this place lieth interred
> The body of Mr. FRANCIS DIXON of Watton
> who departed this life May 1 1722. Aged 28 Years.
> He married REBECCA eldest daughter of
> THOMAS SHUCKFORTH of Saham Gentleman:
> by whom he had Issue 4 children
> THOMAS, FRANCIS, MARY. And JOHN
> JOHN died an infant THOMAS died April 19 1737
> In the 20th Year of his Age
> MARY (who married to her first Husband
> Mr. JOHN CARTER of London, by whom
> She had no issue, and to her Second
> Husband the Revd. Mr. THOMAS ARCHER
> of Finchley in Middlesex by whom she had issue, one son named
>   THOMAS)
> She died June 23 1772
> Aged 48 Years.
> Also the body of REBECCA eldest Daughter
> Of the above mentioned Mr. THOMAS SHUCKFORTH
> And Relict of Mr. AMBROSE PAIN of Houghton
> (her Second Husband)
> She departed this Life May 31.1773.
> Aged 82 Years.

Mary had lived just long enough to see her son gain his BA, dying a year before her mother. Unlike his ancestors, Thomas would attain no further academic qualifications. We can only speculate as to whether Mary was well enough to have attended Thomas's ordination as a deacon in Trinity College on Trinity Sunday, 14 June, 1772, by Bishop John Peterborough. Meanwhile, Thomas himself had immediate need of a job, since all the family money was now gone. With the confidence of youth, he turned to gambling, convinced he would recover his fortune. In this he was probably aided and abetted by his Uncle Francis, whose downhill path through gambling dogged his own life. Francis died in 1781, whereupon the huge size of his debts was revealed, and in 1784 the House of Lords passed an Act of Parliament compounding those debts.

The job Thomas found was that of an assistant schoolmaster – usher – of Bury St Edmund's Free Grammar School. It was in this vulnerable time that he must have fallen in love with a lady from Peterborough, but having no money and no clear prospects the couple realised that they had little chance of gaining permission to marry, especially as she was under 21. At which point they decided to elope, and a dramatic chase across the countryside ensued as the irate father and two of his friends pursued them, waving pistols. Once caught, the unhappy pair had no option but to give up their plan, but the young lady told her father she was determined to marry Thomas once she was of age in a year's time. An article in *The Cambridge Chronicle* for 11 September, 1773, describes Archer as a *"smart fellow of the turf"* and, more mockingly, *"the turf hero"*. Apparently, his schoolmastering had not had a sobering effect on his leisure tastes, and his addiction to hunting, racing and gambling had continued after his mother's death. Running away was not only a romantic bid to wed Eliza but also a fleeing from his debtors. On his enforced return to Cambridge, Thomas was clapped into the castle prison where he must languish until his debts were paid, like a character in a Hogarth cartoon. However, he shortly underwent a prodigal-son moment and returned to his senses, contrite and penitent.

The very next week, *The Cambridge Chronicle* published his poem, *An Elegy to Resignation.* This is the first of several of Archer's surviving poems and it shows him to be a creative and artistic wordsmith, if somewhat stereotypical in his sentiments. Thus, the seventh stanza:

> My wounded heart thou sweet Physician heal
> Deign o'er my soul to shed thy balm divine
> For ah! the pangs I've felt, the pangs I feel
> Yield to no pow'r, or only yield to thine.

Perhaps he was paid a little for it, and certainly when he submitted it to *The Gentleman's Magazine* nine years later (August 1782) it must have earned him a welcome addition to his finances. In debtors' prison, he came to realise that his gift of poetry could be a financial boost as well as a leisure pursuit.

There are no records from this time relating to the prison, and we do not know exactly what conditions prevailed for Thomas. The fact that he managed to write a poem and send it for publication in his first week in gaol suggests that his imprisonment was not of the worst kind. Indeed, the old Norman castle in which he was held was known to have better conditions than the local borough gaol. As to how and when he settled his debts and escaped from prison, we can only speculate. The wider family must have been aware of his need, and the wealthy Stonestreets could well have assisted. The 50 guineas that Thomas Stonestreet bequeathed in 1775 was, after all, the equivalent of a year's wages for a curate. But Rebecca Stonestreet's will of 1794, paying off Thomas's debts, suggests he remained unreliable with money.

Amongst Thomas's ordination papers, now held in the Guildhall Library, there is a copy of his baptism certificate. It is dated 19 February, 1774, and was obtained, no doubt, as one of the papers he needed to be priested by the Bishop of London. The date indicates that he was either still in prison or had recently been freed when he began to pursue his priesting. In the event, it was another five years before this finally took place. Maybe he or the authorities felt that the ignominy of his wildness and bankruptcy should be well forgotten before hands were again laid upon him. But by 1775 he was functioning as a curate in a variety of Essex parishes, where news of his dubious past would have been unlikely to have reached.

In local Essex mythology, tales abound of a colourful and dandily-dressed parson madly galloping from church to church each Sunday in order to fulfil his obligations to the parishioners in each locality he was covering, officially or unofficially. Danbury, Canvey Island, and South Benfleet are included in these stories, but sticking strictly to the evidence, the following reconstruction can be made of the first 40 years of his ministry, in which he was caught up in the vicissitudes and lifestyle of an unbeneficed curate of Trollopian dimensions.

In 1775, he became curate of North Benfleet in Essex, then part of the London Diocese. This date comes from his own letters, but the arrangement appears to have been recorded only retrospectively in the bishop's registers:

"Mr. Archer lives in the Parsonage of North Benfleet for the use of which, together with 10 acres of Glebeland he pays £12 p.a. He receives £30 for serving North Benfleet, £30 for serving Rawreth and £25 for serving Hockley."

The registers note that Rawreth is a more eligible place to live than North Benfleet, although Thomas is apparently still living in the same parsonage some years later. The rector of North Benfleet was John Warner, who had been appointed on 22 March, 1775, so he must have employed Thomas as his curate almost immediately after his institution. According to the ODNB, Warner's own appointment was said to be a response to the complaints of his clergyman father that his son was not being sufficiently recognised.

John Warner himself had studied at Trinity Cambridge, and although he was older than Thomas their paths would have crossed there. Moreover Warner, like Archer, was an eccentric and sympathetic to his plight, offering him the curacy at Benfleet. Thomas lived in the parsonage house there whilst the rector spent most of his time writing and travelling. He was a Francophile who got caught up in the French Revolution, which he initially supported. Thus, he spent the winter of 1778/9 in Paris, where he also became chaplain to the British ambassador, and where his sister was a French nun.

Warner was a friendly, caring man, and for all his privileges helped relieve the distresses of his poor parishioners. He was described as moderate at the table and abstemious at the bottle; a book, a pipe, and cheerful conversation were his delight. He was a Whig and a reformer. It is easy to see how such a man not only gave Thomas his first clerical job opportunity, but also provided a model of compassion and care for his ministry.

Neighbouring Hockley had an interregnum in 1776, which Thomas appears to have covered. The next rector, Henry Rigby, already had parishes near Cambridge so Thomas continued to assist him at Hockley. Thomas was also curate to Dr John Wilgress, rector of Rawreth, who was a scholar and preacher but lived on his own estate at Eltham in Kent. Meanwhile, in 1778 Warner resigned as rector of North Benfleet and Samuel Trenoweth replaced him, but he too was an absentee vicar, living at Chesham in Bucks. So Trenoweth continued to employ Thomas to run his parish. Thus, during this time, Thomas was serving and juggling three churches as a curate but still as a deacon.

On the strength of having a home and an income, Thomas was ready to begin family life. Sometime in 1776 he must have married, but was it to the bewitching Eliza? Apparently not, unless Eliza had been a pseudonym, for his new wife was called Ann and, during 1777, she gave birth to a son, Thomas. Meanwhile, in order to take steps to obtaining his own living, Thomas first needed to be ordained as a priest. Presumably his curacies had simply not had communion services, or perhaps their rectors turned up occasionally to preside.

On 22 January, 1779, Thomas wrote to the Bishop of London apologising that he couldn't afford to come and see him personally, but enquiring about what paperwork was required for his priesting. Interestingly, he now describes himself as curate of Rawreth, whose incumbent steps forward to support his request for priesting, since the next letter in the ordination papers is from Dr Wilgress at Eltham to the Bishop of London, dated 6 February, 1779. It is supportive of Thomas, but suggests that there may be a problem contacting his vicar at North Benfleet, since John Warner was travelling in France and not available for a reference.

"Sir, as I find by Dr. Eaton's letter that you think a title necessary for a person taking the office of priest as well as that of deacon and fearing Mr. Archer by some accident may be disappointed of procuring a title from the rector of the adjoining parish whose church he also serves and in whose parsonage he resides... (I declare) Mr. Archer has behaved unexceptionably since he became my curate for the space of three years past and I should be extremely concerned if anything should operate to his disadvantage in obtaining the sacred office for which I think him duly qualified. Pray tendre my compliments to Dr. Eaton and believe me to be, Sir, your most humble servant."

The letter was well-pitched. Wilgress's familiarity with the bishop's secretary was assumed but not over-stated. And his own acknowledgement of the sanctity of the sacred office emphasised his concern for the honour of the church and its servants. He refrained from saying how inconvenient it would be for him if Thomas was not priested. The letter did the trick, and three concerned absentee incumbents not only kept their curate but also had the peace of mind that he would henceforth celebrate Holy Communion on their behalf.

Thomas needed three referees, who were Wilgress himself; Daniel Halloway, rector of Foulness; and William Cropley, of West Ham, all of whom testified to having observed Thomas for three years and believed him worthy of priesting. So, on 28 February, 1779, Thomas travelled to London to be priested in the Royal Chapel, St James's Palace. He was also officially licensed as curate of North Benfleet for a stipend of £35 pa and Rawreth at £40 pa; at this point, he appears to have dropped Hockley.

Then, just when his life seemed more settled, tragedy struck again. His wife died and was buried at North Benfleet on 17 October. The local story is that he drove the coffin to the church himself and then took the service rather than asking a neighbouring clergyman, as was conventional. His remembered words were quoted by a local historian, Philip Benton:

"Good bye. God bless you. You were a good wife. Farewell. Thank God who has enabled me to do this. I dare say there will be observations made, but by not employing a brother clergyman I have saved the fees and a hatband."

If he had been a mourner, convention dictated formal dress, including a hatband. By robing as the officiating minister, he avoided that formality and expense. Was this tongue-in-cheek or honest, blunt speaking? Honesty, deep feeling, faith, and humour combine in these few words. But with a two-year-old to care for and without wider family support, he unsurprisingly married again swiftly. More surprisingly, the marriage bond reveals that it was to Susannah Page, the 18-year-old daughter of John Page of Nevendon, who was an illiterate farm labourer. Susannah too was illiterate, whilst her husband-to-be was competent in Latin and Greek.

From a preferment viewpoint, young Mrs Archer could not have been much of a help to Thomas's prospects, but the marriage was apparently a success and lasted more than 50 years. They wed at North Benfleet on 7 January, 1780, although somewhat incongruously the licence – necessary since Susannah was underage – is dated 17 January![1] The trauma of Ann's death and the ensuing romance with Susannah seems to have reminded him of his poem from prison, *Resignation,* which was successfully published in *The Gentleman's Magazine* of August 1782.

In 1783, the family managed to make a move into the "better part of Essex", as Thomas himself describes it. He was to become curate of South Church on the Essex coast. The rector was Walter Wren Driffield, who had taken his BA at Trinity College in the same year that Thomas arrived there, so their paths would have crossed. The community at Trinity would have been aware of the trauma the young undergraduate underwent with his father's death and of his slipping off the rails. Some would have been judgmental, but some would have felt compassion and Driffield seems to have been one of them. Since leaving Trinity, Driffield had done well for himself and been rector of South Church since 1774. He was also chaplain to the Cornwallis family and married well – to Elizabeth Townshend, daughter of the Very Revd. Hon Viscount Townshend.

His other significant achievement was that he had been called upon to baptise John Constable in the night, for Constable had been a sickly child, not expected to live. Driffield maintained a lifelong friendship with the artist and his family, and indeed introduced the Archers to him. Although Thomas moved to South Church in 1783, he does not seem to appear in the archbishop's records (South Church being an Archbishop's Peculiar) until much later. Instead, the evidence of his 1783 appointment comes from the parish registers. When Thomas arrived, he found those registers were full, but squeezed into a remaining space a few telling lines:

> "There being no register of baptisms and burials since? This old one being filled up when I undertook the cure of souls at South Church at Michelmas 1783. The following which I have enur'd are entered as a memorandum till a new register be procured. T. Archer Curate."

About the same time, he also became linked with the neighbouring parish of Prittlewell, where his signature begins to appear in their registers. His signature is intermittent, which would indicate that he was helping at Prittlewell sporadically. However, all his children were baptised at Prittlewell, suggesting that that is where the family actually lived.

Mary Ann was born and baptised in 1786, named after Thomas's mother and first wife.

Benjamin Maurice, named after Thomas's grandfather Benjamin, was baptised in 1788.

Susan, named after her mother, was born and baptised in 1792.

In 1796, their next child, Edward, named after Thomas's great grandfather, did not live for long. Thomas reverted to Latin in the register, perhaps echoing his sense of solemn grief:

"son of Thomas, clerk and Susannah uxoris"

The following year, Catherine was baptised and the Latin retained. Named after his only cousin, she is described as "filia Thomas et Susan".

Meanwhile, Thomas found himself covering the parish of Little Wakering during an interregnum, and consequently deciding to make a bid to become the next rector. The patronage belonged to St Bartholomew's Hospital, whose governors made the appointment by ballot. However, Thomas was all too aware that he was an unknown curate, too poor to travel to London to lobby the governors, which put him at a great disadvantage. His only hope was his written eloquence and the support of someone important. The trouble was he did not now meet many important people.

His best bet was the second Earl of Hardwicke, a friend of his late uncle. The letter is dated 11 June, 1788. Thomas introduces himself as the nephew of Francis Dixon, receiver general of Cambridge, who, he says, once described the earl as his best friend. He recounts his misfortunes; the early death of his father and, more recently that of his Uncle Francis, as well as the loss of the family fortune. He had been a curate now for nearly 14 years but had recently applied to the governors of St Bartholomew's Hospital, the patrons of Little Wakering where he was currently standing in as curate. Might the earl be able to champion his application? Whether he did or didn't, Thomas failed to get the job.

Not until 1790 is there a diocesan record of his position at Prittlewell, even though he had been working there for eight years. Indeed, one of the results of following Thomas's career path in detail is to expose the laxity of the late Georgian church. The bishop was far away in London, and had little time or resolve to keep tabs on small Essex churches. Archdeacons and absentee clergy drifted round the continent, leaving the weekly servicing of such churches to curates, who seem to have been sincere and humble. Like Thomas, they got on with making arrangements with rectors to provide for small parishes on agreed terms. Sometimes these arrangements were never formalised, and others were authorised retrospectively.

On 27 May of that year, we have the record of Thomas being licensed as curate at £25 pa. The current rector was Sir Herbert Croft, a priest, a baronet, and an author. He was best known for his novel *Love and Madness,* which is based on a true story about the passion of a soldier-turned-clergyman for the mistress of the Earl of Sandwich, who was shot by her lover as she was leaving Covent Garden in 1779. Croft had matriculated at University College, Oxford in March 1771, and subsequently entered Lincoln's Inn. He was called to the bar, but in 1782 returned to Oxford with a view to preparing for holy orders. In 1786, he received the vicarage of Prittlewell, but he remained at Oxford for some years, accumulating materials for a proposed English dictionary. He was twice married, and on the day after his second wedding day, he was imprisoned at Exeter for debt. He then retired to Hamburg, and two years later his library was sold, for although he had inherited the title of baronet he did not inherit the estates and wealth that went with it.

Ironically, he was descended from the Archers of Umberslade, from which gentry family Thomas Archer is said, by Benton, to have claimed descent with no evidence to support him! Croft returned briefly to England in 1800, but went abroad once more in 1802 and died in Paris in 1816. Although he was mostly absent from his parish, in one version of his poem about Southend, Thomas extols saintly Herbert's benevolence and gifts to the poor of the parish.

Near Prittlewell was the seaside hamlet of Southend, which had been growing in reputation as a bathing place conveniently near London. More and more bathing machines appeared on the beach as hotels and boarding houses were spreading. An entrepreneur, Thomas Holland, laid down a plan for a gentrified new town named New Southend. Thomas Archer basked in the reflected glory. In the Prittlewell registers for 1793, he recorded the baptism of one "John Mitchell (of NEW SOUTHEND) being the first child born there". The second such child was also recorded, but after that the novelty wore off. Meanwhile, Thomas extolled the virtues of the new town in an extended poem with a prolix 18th century title:

Poetical Description of New South-End in the county of Essex and its vicinitys

Just over 300 perfectly metred lines in rhyming couplets reveal the hand of a skillful poet. The classical allusions are not overdone, but ally a romanticism about Essex with the Arcadian beauty of the ancients. But there are plentiful modern descriptions of carriages, bathing machines, grand hotels, and a library, that make the newly-emerging New Southend a match for Weymouth, Margate or Brighthelmstone (Brighton). France, across the water, is aflame with destructive revolutionary fervour, but Southend epitomises the gentle and just ways of England and her monarchy, as reflected in the languid Thames bearing trade and pleasure to and from her shores.

There were two editions of the poem. The first was in 1793, and it is this one that lauds Thomas's absentee rector and his generosity to the poor. In the second, 1794 edition, it is Thomas Holland the entrepreneurial and speculative architect of New Southend whose plaudits are newly inserted in Herbert's place:

Thy lib'ral hand has no expence deny'd

An anonymous reviewer for the *Gentleman's Magazine* visited Southend and purchased a copy of the first edition of the poem, which he rapturously reviewed in June 1794.[2] At one shilling a copy, Thomas must have considered that his luck was in and a future as a poet lay before him. However, two clouds were already on the horizon – the first being that Thomas Holland went bankrupt the following year, and New Southend's glorious future went on hold.

The second was the aftermath of the anonymous reviewer's visit to Mr Rennison's commodious shop in Southend, where he purchased Archer's poem. On the way out, Mrs Rennison, with a quick eye to a further sale, informed the gentleman that Archer had just published another poem: *The Triumph of Loyalty*, in which Thomas really gets into his stride against the French, evoking the story of Daniel and his friends as models of the heroic English character. The reviewer is clearly not as enamoured with his second purchase, especially as the price had risen to half a crown. He thought it rushed and unpolished in comparison with the first successful poem. Nevertheless, he quotes extensively from *The Triumph*, giving posterity the only record of this particular poem.

New Southend is an upbeat and celebratory local poem in its own right, but it is also haunted by the events going on across the channel, almost within sight of the Essex coast; the French revolution was in full swing and Thomas, radical in many things, was both patriotic and conservative in his condemnation of its cruelty, bloodshed, atheism, and destruction of the social order. Thomas arranged collections in both Great Wakering and Prittlewell for the French priests, Roman Catholic as well as protestant, who had fled to England in the wake of the revolution.[3]

On 18 November, 1794, Archer was belatedly licensed as curate to the parish of Southchurch, for which it was agreed that the rector would pay him £45 pa.

Presuming it reached him, Thomas now received another legacy, this time for £20. More than the money was the poignant bequest of his mother's watch and seal. It came from a Norfolk lady, Susanna Bodham, who had been very close to his parents. The wording speaks for itself. "I give to that unhappy young man… Archer now or late of Benfleet… as a token of my great affection for his parents."

Thomas was reminded how far short of his esteemed parents he had fallen. Someone from their world dimly remembered him, had lost track of his moves, perhaps forgotten his Christian name, but sent him tokens from the world he could have inhabited as a Norfolk vicar, perhaps.

In 1798, a bald statement appears in the Prittlewell registers: *The curate resigns.*

Quite why remains unclear, but it is probable that his rector, Croft, was returning to live in the parish and vicarage, so Thomas would be redundant and homeless. But it could equally well be to do with money. The parish he took on to replace Prittlewell was 10 miles away in Pitsea. When he was finally licensed there in 1814 [almost 14 years since he first worked there!], he was paid £50 pa, twice what he had received at Prittlewell.

Money certainly remained an issue, as he now had five children to feed, clothe, and educate. Three were girls, and their marriage prospects would be much enhanced if he could amass some money. Two more patriotic poems followed: *The Battle of Aboukir*, 1799, and *The Victory of Copenhagen*, 1801, rushed out after Britain had defeated a Danish Navy, newly allied with the French. It seems that he hoped these would appeal to the English heart, sell well, and make some cash. They do not survive.

A more reflective Archer poem of 1802 does survive. It was not ever published, and was composed for the funeral of his neighbour in Sutton, Revd. Henry Ellis: it caught the picture of the gentleman curate, a scholar who lacked contacts and, like Thomas, survived as a curate unable to obtain a parish of his own. Ellis laboured faithfully among his flock for many years.

> He gave to misery all he had, a Tear
> He gained from Heaven the Boon he wished, a Friend
> At length kind Providence a Patron rais'd
> Who independence, ease and comfort gave.

So it was that Thomas continued patiently to trust that kind Providence would soon provide him with a patron and a parish. Meanwhile, there was a smile from heaven in the form of a more substantial inheritance from his cousin Catherine, who died in 1803, classified as a lunatic, leaving him as next of kin a small farm in Somerset. The consistory court of London valued the property at £2,000.[4]

Another encouragement was the visit of Princess Charlotte, aged five, to Southend. In the week, she bathed in the sea every day for her health's sake but on Sunday she attended Southchurch where Thomas Archer was presiding. It was his granddaughter who passed on the story which no doubt she had regaled to her by her proud grandfather.

Perhaps inspired by his brush with royalty and in spite of the new farm, ever in need of higher income, he returned to the thought of a major patriotic poem, and what could be more inspiring than Nelson's recent victory at Trafalgar to tug at British heart strings and pockets. This time, he proposed to raise the money to print such a poem from subscriptions, and this he began to do with some success. Once he had some impressive names behind him, he decided to go straight to the top and wrote to the Prime Minister, Lord Grenville, in his usual anecdotal style on 8 February, 1806:

"May it please your Lordship to pardon my presumption in troubling your Lordship with this address – I beg your leave to state that I am a clergyman professed of a small income: barely adequate to the maintenance of a numerous family. I dedicate my vacant hours chiefly to poetry and have published several poems with considerable success.

I shall shortly bring forth a poem in honour of the immortal memory of our late deceased Naval Hero, the Illustrious admiral Lord Nelson, whose Praise is the theme of every Tongue. This intended publication has met with patronage, which exceeds my merits and my hopes. His Grace the Duke of Bedford, Earl and Countess Temple, and many other exalted characters have condescended to become subscribers. My design is more fully explained, and a few of the chief subscribers set down, on the other side of this paper. With the most profound submission, I humbly request to be honoured with your Lordships highly respectable Name as a subscriber to this work; in the conclusion of which a tribute will be paid to the memory of the late Marquis Cornwallis and Mr Pitt. While every patriotic bosom rejoices in your Lordships appointment to the Helm of State, permit me to join in the general acknowledgement of your Lordships integrity and abilities and express my fervent wish and hope that the welfare of our glorious Constitution may be preserved, and established under your wise counsel and direction as a statesman; meantime I remain with the highest consideration your Lordships dutiful servant

Thomas Archer, Curate of this parish 24 years."

The Battle of Trafalgar or Victory and Death Sacred to the immortal memory of the late illustrious Naval Hero Admiral Lord Nelson shortly will be published by subscription. Price Four Shillings. A poem by the Rev. T. Archer BA, author of *The Triumph of Loyalty, The battle of Abakiri, the Victory of Copenhagen* and various other poems.

> He then lists his principal subscribers:
> His Grace the Archbishop of Canterbury, 5 copies
> The Duke of Bedford, 10; The Duke of Grafton, 5
> The Rt. Honourable Earl & Countess Temple, 2
> Lord Barham, 2; The Lord Wodehouse, 3; Lady L Harvey, 2
> Rt Revd. Lord Bishops of Winchester, 4; London, 3; Lincoln,
>   2; Chichester, 2; Bath & Wells, 2; Chester, 2; Durham, 1
> 4 MPs, ordering 10 between them.
> And a great number of nobility and gentry and clergy, to the
>   amount of some hundreds of copies.

We have no knowledge of whether Grenville joined the subscribers, but as the letter survived amongst his papers he may well have read it and responded. From the sums suggested in the letter, it looks like Thomas was onto a winner. However, there is no sure evidence I have seen as to whether the poem was ever written or reviewed!

Given that it is bad news that so often gets noticed and recorded, it is unsurprising to have a record left of Southchurch's mad dog crisis. Driffield himself returned to chair the meeting in Southchurch's hour of crisis, though Thomas would inevitably have been involved. Apparently, dogs were so terrorising the villagers that they called a parish meeting to deal with this outbreak of canine madness. This was on 22 March, 1808, and the minutes record that the rector presided, supported by Mr. Saward, churchwarden, farmers, and villagers. They passed four resolutions:

"First, That public notice be given in this village on the alarming crisis occasioned by canine madness and that all inhabitants are requested to chain up or confine their dogs.

"Second, That any person who finds a dog at large in this parish is desired to destroy the animal, on proof of which being made, the person who shall destroy such dog shall be entitled to a reward of one shilling from the churchwarden of this parish."

Then came some nasty threats, because the third resolution read:

"That no poor person who keeps a dog at this perilous time shall receive relief from this parish in any shape whatever.

"Fourth, That in order to discourage the practice of keeping useless and mischievous dogs in this parish, we will not knowingly give employ to any labourer keeping such a dog."

Thomas had to read these resolutions at the church door after divine service, and a copy of them was affixed to the church door and to the blacksmith's shop. He also had to visit the White Horse and the Rose Inn, and read the resolutions to the assembled companies. Did they buy him a drink?

Another village niggle was petty crime, and that same year saw the theft of Thomas's wheelbarrow from Southchurch vicarage.[5] But much more distressing was the onset of his son Benjamin's illness. What it was is not defined, but the tone in which it is discussed suggests a mental health issue.

More positively, Benton records that Thomas produced another poem in praise of a local dignitary, Asser Vassal, also in 1808. But the real good news of that year was the marriage of his eldest daughter Mary Ann, aged 22, to William Stammers, a London clerk, recorded as a widower, but still only 23. How they might have met is a speculative question. Was there a clerks' outing to Southend, or did William have relatives locally? Thomas took the wedding at Southchurch on 27 July. It was witnessed by Susannah Archer – Mary Ann's sister – and John Guiver, who placed his mark. Within a year, Thomas and Susan were grandparents.

Thomas had not given up on the quest for a living, taking us back to those letters in Eton College archives from which this project began. I reproduce the one he sent to the college when the parish of Hitcham became vacant in 1810. It repeats information already given, but Thomas's skill is in presenting his story, and reading an account of his life from his own lips makes the letter an important insight into his life, as well as an informative document about the situation and psychology of an early 19th century clergyman.

> Southchurch Parsonage near Rochford Essex
> December 8 1810
> To the Revd. And worthy society, the Provost, Vice-Provost and Fellows of Eton College
> Revd. Gentlemen,
> With proper deference and respect to your venerable society I humbly offer myself a candidate for the vacant Rectory of Hitcham, to which no one can be presented without your nomination [according to the will of my worthy ancestor Dr. Thomas Evans, Patron of the living and Fellow of Eton who died in the year 1733 and devised the advowson of the church at Hitcham to my grandfather Benjamin Archer and his heirs for ever but likewise directed that no person should be presented to the living at any time, except such person as had a nomination from you]. In consequence of this my father, who was assistant at Eton, was instituted to the living more than seventy years ago, and resigning it sometime after, he obtained much superior Preferment... Dr Evans [who endowed Eton College with the nomination to the living and devised the actual Presentation to my grandfather and his heirs] was own brother to my grandmother; her maiden name was Evans. Dr. Evans and she were the son and daughter

of the Rev. Dr. Evans who possessed large estates in and about Hitcham and was [I think] a Canon of Windsor. My grandmother and my father and his first wife lie buried in the churchyard of Hitcham. I had the honour of being related likewise to Dr. Carter and Dr. Reynolds who I have been informed were fellows of Eton College.

My grandfather was Rector of Quainton, Bucks and my Uncle was Fellow of King's College Cambridge and Rector of Stour Provost, Dorsetshire. My father had the living of Finchley, Middlesex and St. Martin's Ludgate and was a Prebend of St. Paul's Cathedral and also Lecturer of Divinity at the same Cathedral, and all my ancestors [as I have understood] were clergymen for the space of many generations receiving their education at Eton School.

Sed proavos et qua fecunus ipse vise ea nostra voco *[Now as to birth and ancestors and those things which we have ourselves achieved, I scarcely call such distinctions our own – Ovid]*

I had the misfortune to be deprived of the best of fathers when I was only 17 years old, whose tomb bears in Hitcham churchyard [in a Latin inscription] my humble testimonies of his virtues and his patience. He had no private fortune when he died being a younger brother. My mother had a good provision from her own family, but lost it all by an unfortunate failure in London of the person to whom it was entrusted and of course I was left without any income except the emolument arising from the exercise of my sacred profession, though I had the misfortune [for a misfortune I would call it] to be brought up under an expectation of affluence.

Mrs. Catherine Archer, daughter of my father's dear brother, died in the year 1803, at whose death I became profit of a small estate in Somersetshire and all the rights and works of the family as the sole surviving heir of the family. She was for the space of nearly thirty-four years under Guardianship being awfully defective in understanding, and of course could neither conduct her own affairs, nor exercise any trust. My small paternal estate provides a very small annual rent. I never had the happiness of obtaining preferment and my whole life has been a series of disappointments. I am nearly sixty, but through God's mercy enjoy a sound constitution and a very good state of health have been married thirty years to my present wife and have five children, three of whom are dependent upon me for support, and one of my sons has been for two years afflicted with a tedious illness and is not likely ever to be able to earn his maintenance. I have been a curate for thirty-five years and have been minister of this parish nearly thirty years, my other cure is ten miles distant from this place. My whole income [after deducting the expenses of keeping a horse to which I am compelled by the distance of my churches] does not exceed an hundred and thirty pounds annually. And out of this small pittance I am obliged to defray several taxes and if age or infirmity should render me incapable of doing my duty as a clergyman, my situation will then be very awkward.

From this gloomy posture of affairs and still more gloomy prospect of poverty in old age, you gentleman have the power of liberating me and if you will confer on me a nomination to the living that was once entirely the property of my ancestors, you will confer upon me an unspeakable obligation, for which I can never be sufficiently grateful. My conduct if I succeed shall speak my gratitude. I promise to render upon the living and to perform my duty twice every Sunday and my conduct shall never disgrace your patronage.

I have been informed the value of the living is but small, but it is a great object to me as if I can obtain it I shall be ensured of a comfortable asylum during the remainder of my years and shall enjoy the satisfaction of knowing that my bones will repose among the ashes of father, my grandmother, her father and brother all buried at Hitcham. If my request meet with your approbation and my petition be granted it may be remembered that my time of life precludes me from the prospect of being an obstacle [to the views of any person who at present may wish to obtain the living] for any long series of years.

I can at any time if necessary provide strong testimonials of my moral character and as some sort of recommendation I beg permission to present for your perusal a letter with which I was honoured formerly by the late exemplary, pious and benevolent Bishop of London which I beg may be returned. Meantime with an earnest wish for the prosperity of your learned society and profound respect I remain Rev. Gentlemen

Your dutiful servant

How Eton could resist this eloquent appeal, I do not know! I think it unlikely that they remembered his youthful indiscretions, though they may have questioned how he had reached the age of sixty without having a living. Most likely, they already had a man in mind who was currently a Fellow of Eton. Thomas made a brave bid to counter this probability which he must have foreseen, but in vain. In fact, it was the Provost of Eton himself who added Hitcham to his portfolio of parishes. To rub salt into his wound, Thomas was now required to present the new rector of Hitcham, since he remained the legal patron. It was only because his great uncle had stipulated that Eton could choose who was appointed that Thomas could not have appointed himself, as patrons often did.

Much of Thomas Archer's story is archetypal of the period; the poor curate ever in search of a living. His position was not as hopeless as it could have been, since he came from a respected clerical family. However, Thomas had made some basic misjudgments, chiefly that of getting into debt. His father had died before he could secure a position for his son, and Uncle Francis turned out to be a liability and may even have been a cause of leading his nephew astray. Then, Thomas had married a labourer's daughter who would never become a gracious lady of the vicarage. Perhaps the implications of these decisions only came home to him late in life as he realised more clearly how society and the church worked. All the clergy Thomas worked for had mastered the system and were largely absentees from their parishes, thus requiring a curate to run their churches. They took the income to finance their absentee lifestyles and paid their curate a minimal stipend. But the story is not yet over for Thomas.

Meanwhile, he pressed on with another of his literary endeavours, the author of which is revealed only as the writer of *The Triumph of Loyalty*, suggesting that that poem had had greater success than was predicted by his critics.The new poem was a 20-page, 588-line epic describing the heroic endeavours of the British and Spanish against the French: *The Battles of Barrosa and Albuera*, subtitled *Valour and Victory*. Whilst undoubtedly in the heroic vein, he does not downplay war's horrors:

"And show'rs of human gore bedew'd the rock"

Thomas must have read accounts in papers, perhaps in Southend's library, and worked swiftly on dramatising scenes from the battles as though he was an eye-witness. The battles were in March and May 1811, and the poem was written, published and printed before the end of that year. The copy in the British Library does not have a price.

Shortly after this, John Constable visited Southchurch and sketched Hadleigh Castle, a drawing he later turned into a melancholic painting following the death of his wife. During the trip, he was introduced to the Archer family by Walter Driffield, who had combined a visit to his parish with a holiday with Constable. In October 1814, Driffield wrote to Constable with deeply significant news:

> "I was last week at Southchurch, when Miss Archer inquired *very* kindly after you. *He* has got the wretched living of Foulness Island and leaves me on Lady Day. George is off for Lancashire with his bride, I think with every prospect of comfort..."

The tone of the letter is ambivalent. Thomas has managed his parish for 32 years and his moving on must have been an inconvenience, especially since Driffield's clergyman son, George, had found his own parish. And what of Miss Archer? Was he suggesting she fancied Constable, who already had a fiancée? But anyhow, Miss Archer lacked money. Did he mean to be a teasing gossip, or were his words more barbed? But for anyone remotely touched by Thomas's 32 years as a curate, it comes as good news to hear that at the age of 65 he finally has a parish, indeed an island of his own.

The patrons of Foulness were the earls of Nottingham and Winchelsea, and this may be the clue to Thomas's appointment. We are left to imagine the fawning letter, though the style is predictable.

My dear Uncle Benjamin was privileged to be chaplain to your very own ancestor's dear wife. He always spoke highly of your family and their charitable acts, especially their service to the Foundling Hospital that brought benefit to so many poor children. And I often observe [for I live

*just across the water from Foulness] how your Lordship
carries that benevolence into his own generation in his
charitable deeds to the poor of Foulness. I would happily
serve under such a patron…*

If there were such begging letters to the patron, the eighth Earl of
Nottingham and Winchelsea, they have not survived, but this slender
link could have turned the tide. The succeeding Earl, George Finch,
was a serious cricket enthusiast who may or may not have introduced
cricket to Foulness. He is certainly famed for his part in founding Lord's
cricket ground. He was a military man who had fought in the American
War of Independence. He never married, but had an illegitimate son,
also George, who succeeded him as patron in 1826. Thomas Archer
was of a similar age to the ninth Earl, and perhaps appealed to the
eccentric side of his patron. Finch also had a real interest in Foulness,
and organised the building of many houses on the island for the poor.

The institution took place on 26 July, 1815: the year that saw the
defeat of Napoleon and the death of Princess Charlotte, as well as
exceptionally cold temperatures occasioned by a volcano in Indonesia.
There is no record of Thomas having written any poems about such
significant events; settling into his new home and parish at the age of
65 must have consumed his energies. His first sermon at St Mary's was
reputedly from a text in Isaiah 42.12

Let them give glory unto the Lord,
and declare his praise in the islands.

Soon after Thomas arrived in Foulness, the population was 250. Most of
these would be farm-workers, since the island was fertile if windswept.
There was a school, which was inspected by a *Select Committee of the
House of Commons on the Education of the Poor,* who published their
report in 1818. The parish allowed £40 per annum for the instruction

of 30 poor children; and the Earl of Winchelsea added a benefaction of £15 to assist the school, and buy religious books, etc, "and the rector is at the expense of four additional scholars".

As well as supporting this school, Thomas began a Sunday School for the children who were unable to attend the weekday school. Slowly, Foulness – like the rest of England – was growing more literate. By the time of Thomas's death, the population had risen steeply to 630. There was one Daily School, with 12 males and eight females; of whom five were paid for by George Finch, Esq, who allowed £5 per annum, and the remainder of the children by their parents. Also, one Sunday School, attended by 15 males and 10 females, supported by an allowance of £5 per annum from George Finch, Esq, and by subscription from the inhabitants.[6] Thomas and patron in tandem modelled the educational improvements of the day. In 1825, two cottages and a garden near the church were purchased by the parish as a workhouse, and remained so until the 1837 reforms. Thomas would have played a key role in establishing this safety net for the poor on Foulness.

On one subject the sources are understandably silent. What was Thomas's attitude towards smuggling? Foulness was perfectly situated for landing illicit cargoes and using the network of small channels that existed around the island to disseminate the booty to the mainland. There were clergy known for their sympathy with the local smugglers, but no hint of this exists for Thomas. Churches were favourite storage spaces for goods unloaded in the dead of night. Thomas could not possibly have been ignorant of this trade, but probably chose to turn a blind eye to it rather than getting actively involved. In return, he may have received a bottle or two.

Meanwhile, the Stammers family of Hackney in East London was steadily growing. Mary Ann was the only child of Thomas and Susan to have a family. William Stammer's Bank of England salary enabled them to support a growing family, and children now appeared every two years. Only Henry Alfred had been brought to Southchurch to be baptised by his grandfather in 1813, whilst all the other children, bar one, were baptised at St Leonard's, Shoreditch. Arabella Clementina may have been a sickly child, since she had an emergency baptism after her birth in 1821.

At this juncture, William senior was made redundant from the Bank but given a pension. He worked next as a carpenter and they had two more children. However, by 1831 only two daughters had survived, Selina and Arabella, and about 1824 Mary Ann herself passed away. William found a new partner, Alice Musto, by whom he had a child in 1827, even though he did not marry her until 1834. Such arrangements were not uncommon in the East End at that time.

Thomas and Susan now seem to have taken responsibility for their remaining two grandchildren. One in particular moves into the centre of the story – Arabella Clementina, who appears in the baptism register of Foulness, 27 April, 1823. Thomas's writing is now very big, evidence of his growing problems with his sight. It was deteriorating in the last years of his life, and for his final eight months he was said to be completely blind. He employs the phrase "fully baptised", suggesting that Arabella's emergency baptism was now being supplemented by a proper church baptism, perhaps by immersion. She is recorded as the daughter of Willam and Mary Stammers of nearby Hadleigh. Is this where the couple were staying for a while?

By this time, there was a steam packet service to London three times a week down the Thames, which would have made it much easier for the Stammers to visit Southend. Thomas adds, with some pride, that William is a pensioner of the Bank of England. Maybe Mary Ann was already ill and unable to look after her remaining children, which is why they came to Foulness. In practice, Arabella seems to have been brought up by Thomas's daughter, Susannah, who had recently married an older widower, William Gardner, a bailiff or yeoman of Pear Tree Farm on nearby Havengore Island. Maybe they realised they were not to have children of their own and the Stammers agreed to give them custody of Arabella.

None of the other Archer children had any children of their own. Thomas wed in 1824 at Finchingfield, Essex, where he had become the schoolmaster. Catherine married a London merchant, Samuel Archer Pearce in 1825, but died a few months later, perhaps in childbirth. The inscription on her gravestone in Prittlewell churchyard simply stated:

"Catherine Pearce aged 27 years, wife of Samuel Pearce a tradesman in London and daughter of Rev Thomas Archer formerly curate of this parish and of Susannah his wife. Also Edward Archer who died in 1796, son of Rev Thomas Archer."

It was about 30 years since baby Edward had died, but Thomas must have had returning memories of his lost son as he returned to Prittlewell for the burial of Catherine. There was a positive codicil to this brief marriage, in that Samuel was also 'fully baptised' by Thomas Archer at Foulness on 18 April, 1826, using the service *for those of riper years.*

Catherine's death was the first of a series of family tragedies. The only other surviving Archer son, Benjamin Maurice, died at the age of 37, unmarried. In May, he and his father were both signatories to a local farmer's will. In October, he drowned in a ditch. Given the guarded comments about his health, one wonders whether this was purely an accident.

An undoubted accident was the drowning of William Gardiner, who was apparently quite deaf. Benton describes dramatically how William died losing his way home on a dark night, unable to hear the cries of those who saw that he was wandering off the safe causeway home.

Susannah Gardiner now found herself a widow and homeless, since the Gardiners had lived in a tied cottage. At this point, she returned to live in the Vicarage at Foulness with young Arabella, bringing the laughter and tears of a young child back into the Vicarage. Meanwhile, the anecdotes that have been passed down about Thomas continue to depict a colourful and upbeat parson. Indeed, there are many stories about Thomas Archer that are still included in local histories today:

Galloping between services as he regularly did, he used to tuck his sermon under his hat. One day, he met a lady and gallantly swept the said hat from his head so that his sermon blew away. Nevertheless, he managed an excellent extempore one.

During a marriage service, the local hunt passed through the churchyard: Thomas cried out 'Tally Ho!' several times in the middle of the wedding service before continuing.

He frequently used to say the blessing as he walked down the aisle, finishing it just as he reached the door, whereupon, leaping on his horse, he galloped away to his next service.

If the hunt was out midweek and he was taking a service, he would wear his scarlet jacket under his surplice, ready to join the chase as soon as the service was over. The hunting pink was inclined to appear through the surplice!

Unlike the sober black worn by his brother clergy, his normal attire consisted of a blue frock coat, white corduroy breeches, and grey worsted stockings without gaiters.

Thomas would walk to church smoking his long clay pipe, where he would knock out the ash, refill the pipe, and place it in a niche in the porch ready for when he came out.

The rambling vicarage at Foulness had no bells and perhaps no full-time servants. So, when Thomas needed something, he would bang the hearth brush loudly against the wainscot calling 'Pug, Pug', which was apparently his wife's nickname.

When he grew too old to go hunting, he took to reading novels which he obtained from Southend library. As his sight began to fail, he needed to keep the candle as close to the page as possible. As more and more library books were returned singed and blackened, the library began to charge him for them.

He was known for his daring on horseback even when he lived on Foulness, and it was whilst trying to leap a 5-bar gate that he fell and broke his leg, so that he was laid up for some weeks. A curate was posted to help him from the mainland, who had to swim his horse to reach the rectory.

Foulness was well-known for bare-knuckle fighting, since its isolation meant the authorities could not easily interfere. The ground in front of the George and Dragon was the arena, in full view of the rectory, where *The Infant, The Giant,* and *Bullock Bones* went at it. There are near-contemporary stories of Archer joining in, but by 2013 a Southend journalist, Ken Westell, in *Tales of the Town*, tells us that "Their parson Tom Archer was a renowned bare-knuckle fighter"! I think that unlikely, though I can imagine him having a round or two of play fighting with the big boys.

These stories are of particular interest in a study of oral history. I think most of them were originally collected by Phillip Benton and written into his *History of the Rochford Hundred,* which he first published in 1867. Benton was seventeen when Thomas died and would have known him personally, listening to the old man's slightly embellished stories.

Benton himself was born in North Shoebury, and would grow up to be not only a traditional gentleman farmer but also the historian of this tip of Essex. Nevertheless, he was not always careful in substantiating his sources, and his work has given rise to a number of inaccuracies that have passed into local folklore along with the authentic stories. There were other locals, older than himself, who still remembered the doings of the eccentric Rector of Foulness. Benton would have been collecting his material well before he published in 1867. In particular, he acknowledges that some of his information came from Thomas's granddaughter, Arabella. However, she was only twelve when Thomas died, so her memories are those of a child. But she may have had some written sources because the date of her great-grandfather's appointment to Hitcham, for example, is correct to the day. But generally, her grasp of detail is somewhat hazy.

Nevertheless, through the mists of time there emerges a rounded character whose personality is vividly depicted, giving us a view of the Archer genes that moulded the Archer character over the centuries. Thomas Archer himself certainly became an eccentric, but he was not necessarily born one. Eccentricity may have developed as a protection from the testing circumstances that befell him. The struggle of being a Cambridge graduate of good background who could not get a living, needed a defence mechanism of a deep nature. Just like the famed cockney sense of humour, eccentricity is a way of coping with the harsher side of life. Romantic poetry being another compensation. Furthermore, his quirkiness was also a weapon of attack upon the established interests that so often lacked compassion and concern.

It seems that there was one more poem left in Thomas after he gained the security of his own living, and that was *Age and Honour or A Tribute to the sacred memory of a beloved and lamented sovereign,* which was his response to the death of King George III in 1820. This was the monarch Thomas had known and prayed for from his childhood who, in spite of bouts of mental illness, had been a figurehead and a family man, modelling Christian morality to the nation. His reign had seen the loss of the American colonies and the defeat of French Republicanism. No doubt these were the themes Thomas warmed to in his rhyming lines, but no copy of his work is known to exist today. As with all his other lost poems, there may well be copies lurking in some attic or country library, but for now our evaluations of his work must rest on those that are known.

Much of the anxiety of remaining an unbeneficed curate for so long had to do with security about the future, which was something Thomas had expressed in his letter to Eton. Once secure in a living, a parson could stay there until his death, whilst an ageing curate could have their agreement terminated at any point the vicar chose. But that was not the end of his worries about the future, since his wife was ten years younger than himself and likely to outlive him. What provision could he make for her future? And that of Susan Gardiner? Then there were Selina and Arabella Stammers, who also depended on him, and yet all of them would lose their home when he died.

Concern for the livelihood of children and grandchildren concern most people contemplating their demise, but for the clergy the need to provide housing for their dependents becomes a powerful motivation, and Thomas embarked on a series of deals to safeguard the future of his family. In 1826, he purchased three acres of land and a farmhouse locally, by auction at The Kings Head, 'to whom the lord delivered by seizin through the rod'. In 1831, he settled a new tenant into his Chew Magna estate, and that same year he made his will.

Meanwhile, Eton were continuing to pursue their interest in the Hitcham advowson, having decided once and for all to sort out its ambiguities before the old man Thomas Archer passed away. To this end, they employed their own solicitor and drew up a complicated legal document for Thomas to sign, in which he surrendered all interest of the Archer family in the advowson. Their first move was to soften him up by sending him a Christmas present in 1831. Then they wrote again, asking whether he was ready to surrender the advowson, which letter crossed with one to them from Thomas.

When he did receive their letter, he wrote again. As he explains, he cannot now see well enough to write so he is dictating to his daughter Susannah. He has at least educated all his children, the women as well as the men. He tells them that he is 'hastening to the grave' and gets a niggle off his chest by acknowledging that the advowson has been 'a source of much trouble' to his family for 99 years! He refers to past litigation on the issue, but no evidence of this is left in Eton's archives or his own papers. He is willing to sign over the advowson but thinks 'it would be an act worthy of the learned, illustrious and benevolent society to settle an annuity of 20lb.[sic] per annum on a poor old clergyman whose family have for so long been intimately connected with the society'! The poor old clergyman has lost nothing of his skill with the pen, nor his cheek, but his daughter's secretarial skills left much to be desired!

The letter is dated 11 January. On 14 January, he performed his last baptism, and on 17 February he died. The Instrument of Resignation to Eton remained unsigned. The advowson now passed to his eldest son, Thomas of Finchingfield.

It only remains to wrap up the story of the Revd. Thomas Archer of Foulness and also that of five generations of clergy named Archer. The immediate family gathered with the solicitor, Michael Comport, for the reading of the will:[7] Michael Comport himself and John Grabham, a distinguished but down to earth local surgeon, described by Thomas as his friends, were the trustees of the estate which was to look after Susannah in her lifetime then be split between Susan Gardiner, his remaining daughter, and the surviving Stammers children.

There are also notes made by the solicitor concerning worries raised by the family. Would he make sure Mr. Grabham attends the funeral? Should the pallbearers wear scarves, hatbands and gloves, or hatbands and cloaks? Mr. Comport will write to Mr. Archer of Finchingfield about that. What time is allowed by the bishop for Mrs Archer to remain in the Rectory? Does Mr. Comport think Mr. Archer might try and take possession of the estate? They would like Mr. Atkinson, Vicar of Canewdon, to take the funeral service. Benton describes Atkinson as a hearty Yorkshireman with a passionate concern for justice, who once asked the bishop if he thought it fair that his own stipend was but £40 a year whilst the bishop had thousands. Apparently, Atkinson's stipend was raised to 40 guineas! He was a big, muscular man with a hearty handshake, who enjoyed his drink. He certainly seems to have been the right man to take Thomas's funeral; alas, we have no records of what he said then. The cost of a tombstone was also discussed, the result being:

Sacred to the memory of Rev. Thomas Archer, rector of
this parish who departed this life the 17 February 1832
aged 82 years. A friend of the poor

Those poignant few words tell the story of a comfortably-off young
man from an established clergy family, whose life encountered tragedy,
sometimes from his own fault and sometimes not. Unable to get a
comfortable living, he ended up living amongst poor folk rather than
rich. In doing so, he probably developed a greater empathy with his
people than any of his predecessors. He also left more traces of his
inner life and spiritual values in his poems and letters than any other
Archer.

The church where Thomas was buried in Foulness [The Virgin
Mary, St. Thomas the martyr and All Saints], with its wooden spire and
fireplace to keep out the worst of Foulness weather, was demolished
in 1850. Thomas's tombstone was incorporated into the chancel of
the new church, where it remains to this day. The two Susannahs, his
widow and daughter, together with 12-year-old Arabella Stammers,
moved into Rochford. Thomas of Finchingfield agreed to sign the
Hitcham advowson to Eton, but also died before it happened. It was
left to their solicitor, Michael Comport, to finalise the deal with Eton,
for which the Archer estate received 10/-! Arabella married a Rochford
shoemaker, William Claydon, and had many children.

In 1839, the widow of schoolmaster Thomas died and her
possessions were auctioned off at Finchingfield.[8] In spite of having
been a mere schoolmaster, without a university education, Thomas and
Magdala's home was a very comfortable, middle class, Victorian abode
with all mod cons. It included books which may just have been his,
or could also have been inherited from his father. The Archer library
was rising again, but had nobody to inherit it after Magdala Archer's
death. It included amongst many others, Hall's Encyclopedia, a Law
Dictionary, Burn's Justice[4 volumes], Pilgrims Progress, The Whole

Duty of Man, a Latin Dictionary, Bibles, An Historical Grammar of the World, and a Life of the comic character Dr.Syntax.

Magdala's death in 1839 ended the Archer name but not the story. The name Archer was used as a Christian name in future generations by both the Stammers and Claydon families. For 150 years, the story lay buried in records and documents, awaiting a Resurrection in a future generation.

Sources

Venn, *Alumni Cantabria*

Philip Benton, *History of the Rochford Hundred* 1888, Text online.

Manorial Court Rolls of Foulness D/DGS M38 pg. 176 (ERO)

The Archer Papers D/DU/514 (ERO)

PCC Wills

ODNB

CCEd

Thomas's Ordination file in the Guildhall Library MS/10326/110.

Parish Registers of Benfleet, Prittlewell and South Church etc. [ERO]

Thomas's letters – *see* Appendix 4

Acts of the Archbishop – Lambeth Palace Library

Notes

1. Marriage Licence ERO D/AEL1780
2. Edition 1 is in the Bodleian; Edition 2 is reproduced by the Southend Historical Soc.
3. Lambeth Palace Library: Returns for the Collection for French Clergy, 1793/4, Lambeth FP Porteus 36 f 193
4. Consistory Court of London, 1803;10
5. Essex Quarter Sessions Q/SP6 33
6. Archer Auction 1839 ERO D/F 35/3/87

Appendix 1:
Thomas Archer's Poems

1773   *Elegy of Resignation*, published in the Cambridge Chronicle 1773, and The Gentleman's Magazine, August 1782.

1793   *Tribute to John Harriot of Broomhills on his Retirement from the Rochford Bench* Benton. No copies.

1794   *A Poetical Description of New Southend.* 1st edition The Bodleian; 2nd Southend Historical Association. Reviewed in the Gentleman's Magazine in August.

       The Triumph of Loyalty. No complete copy but reviewed in the same Gentleman's Magazine where it was copiously quoted.

1799   *The battle of Abakiri.* No copy. Cited in 1806 letter.

1801   *The Victory of Copenhagen.* No Copy. Cited in Benton.

1802   *Elegy to Rev Henry Ellis.* Southend Record Office.

1806   *The Battle of Trafalgar or Victory and Death.* No copy, but letter to Grenville expresses his intention to write it and lists subscribers.

1808   *Tribute to Asser Vassal.* No copy. Possibly to be found in an unnamed local paper. Benton.

1811   *Valour and Victory; the Battles of Barossa and Albuero.* Printed by the author. British Library.

1820   *Age and Honour; a Tribute to a beloved Sovereign.* No copy. Benton.

No date or copy; *The Triumph of Charity.* Benton. This could be an alternative title to one of the above.

How much was Thomas influenced by his contemporary, Wordsworth?
Below is Wordsworth's take on the priests fleeing France.

EVEN while I speak, the sacred roofs of France
Are shattered into dust; and self-exiled
From altars threatened, levelled, or defiled,
Wander the Ministers of God, as chance
Opens a way for life, or consonance
Of faith invites. More welcome to no land
The fugitives than to the British strand,
Where priest and layman with the vigilance
Of true compassion greet them. Creed and test
Vanish before the unreserved embrace
Of catholic humanity:--distrest
They came,--and, while the moral tempest roars
Throughout the Country they have left, our shores
Give to their Faith a fearless resting-place.

Appendix 2:
Publications Containing
Thomas Archer Stories

A History of the Rochford Hundred, Philip Benton, 1888 edition [text online]

Southend on Sea, John William Burrows, 1909 [text online]

Companion to Essex, Herbert Tompkins, Methuen. 1938

Southchurch and its Past, W.Pollitt, 1949

Southchurch a short history, Alfred Goodale [online]

A short guide to the ancient Parish of Southchurch, dedicated to the Holy Trinity

The Origins and Failures of New Southend, Essex Record Office. 1991

Foulness Church Parish Guide. 2000

Essex Eccentrics, Alison Barnes, Essex Libraries. 1987

Islands of Essex, Ian Yearsley, Ian Henry Publications. 2000

A History of Southend, Ian Yearsley, Phillimore. 2001

In Tales of the Town, Ken Westell, Estuary Press. 2013

Appendix 3:
Thomas Archer's Ecclesiastical Career Disentangled!

1772   14.6 Deacon and Usher of Bury St. Edmunds' school, Peterborough. CCEd

1775   Curate of **North Benfleet** – from his correspondence

1776   Curate of North Benfleet, living in the Vicarage. Also curate of **Rawreth** and **Hockley.** Guildhall papers.

1779   28.2. Priested and licensed to North Benfleet and Hockley. Episcopal Acts Book London & CCEd

1782   Curate of **Prittlewell** and **Southchurch**. From the parish registers. Also covering interregnum at **Little Wakering**. [Correspondence with Lord Hardwicke]

1782/3 Signature in registers of **Pitsea** , presumably simply covering an interregnum.

The **Canvey Island** website also claims TA was a curate there at this time, but there is no firm evidence, other than Benton. Maybe he visited informally.

1790   Curate of Prittlewell & **Great Wakering** [Libc] CCEd

1793   Thomas arranged collections in both Great Wakering and Prittlewell for the French priests who had fled to England. [Lambeth FP Porteus 36 f 193]

1794   Curate of Southchurch. [Acts of the Archbishop]

1798   Resigned Prittlewell [registers] and license for Southchurch endorsed. [Acts]

1802   Another endorsement for Southchurch. [Acts]

1805   Letter to Hardwicke says he has two parishes – one 10 miles away, presumably Pitsea, where his signature appears from 1808–14

1814   Curate of **Pitsea** . [Licensing to Pitsea. London. CCEd]

1815   Rector of **Foulness.** [CCEd]

Appendix 4:
Correspondence

Letters to the Bishop are from his ordination papers in the Guildhall library, MS/10326/110

Letter to Lord Hardwicke BL, Add Mss35.625 f179

Letter to Lord Grenville BL, Add Mss71591 f 59

Letters to Eton, quoted with the kind permission of the Dean and Chapter, are in the Hitcham file of Eton's archives. [COLL/CIU.7/1/2]

Driffield's letter to Constable mentioning the Archers. *John Constables Correspondence,* R.B. Beckett, Suffolk Record Society Vol.4. 1962